Identity

A Counter-Formation Guide

First edition August 2023
Design by Jesse Owen, 10AM Design (behance.com/10amdesign) and Fallon Rodgers (fallon-design.com)
ISBN 9798856708171
Published by Frontline Church
www.frontlinechurch.com

Table of Contents

Introduction

Why Counter-Formation?

First, we are constantly being formed. We are far more subject to being influenced than we think. We are not static beings. The environment we live in, what we read and watch, the relationships we engage in, where we go and what we do, are always shaping our desires, our beliefs, and our habits. We are dynamic beings who are always being formed, whether we realize it or not. We can either be formed towards the way of Jesus, or formed away from it. In previous generations, it was common for people to become Christians after inheriting a vast reservoir of Christian teaching. The Christian story had shaped and influenced the institutions in which people were formed. But now people are often unfamiliar with the Bible and unsure of what it means to be human. "Right and wrong" is increasingly determined by what "feels" right or wrong.

Second, the rate of deformation is staggering. In this digital age, technology collectively assaults us with deforming ideas. Technology can be a tool for the common good, and it can be used to spread the good news of Jesus and form people towards him. But we are in an unprecedented moment in human history where each of us are constantly plugged in, constantly consuming, constantly connected. We are continually being fed versions of "the good life" that are usually not true or beneficial. We are surrounded by stories of heroes and villains that unconsciously shape our beliefs. Those subtle stories, those versions of "the good life," are twisting our desires and forming us in directions that are not ultimately for our good.

Third, formation is never passive. Counter-formation will require grace-fueled effort. If we think we can simply float through life and effortlessly become more like Jesus, we are gravely mistaken. The rate of deformation we experience has gone from a lazy river to a raging rapid that is sweeping us off our feet. Increasingly, we have seen people tire of swimming against the cultural current, leading to their departure from the Christian faith. Without thoughtful effort, without new habits, and without true community, we will be swept away by the current. But deformation is neither inevitable nor guaranteed. With the help of the Holy Spirit, we can stand firm against the forces pulling us away from Jesus. By God's grace, we can work to have a life constantly shaped by the way of Jesus. In our age of deformation, we don't have to panic about the darkness of the world. Rather, we trust that Jesus is still at work, transforming his people by his grace.

What Does Counter-Formation Look Like?

> *I appeal to you therefore, brothers, by the mercies of God, to present your bodies as a living sacrifice, holy and acceptable to God, which is your spiritual worship. Do not be conformed to this world, but be transformed by the renewal of your mind, that by testing you may discern what is the will of God, what is good and acceptable and perfect.* **Romans 12:1-2**

This passage speaks to us about both deformation and counter-formation. When Scripture says, "Do not be conformed to this world," it is describing deformation. It is warning us against being conformed to the values of the world, the loves of the world, the desires of the world, and the versions of "the good life" that the world presents to us. In contrast, it invites us to "be transformed by the renewal of your mind." This is counter-formation. It is encouraging us to embrace the transforming work of grace—which comes to us through various means in order to shape what we love, believe, and do.

We cannot respond to deformation by recreating an idealized version of the so-called "good old days." Nor can we kick the can down the road and hope that someday discipleship and mission will become easier. Rather, we must renew our minds and present our bodies as living sacrifices. To do that, we must name some of the most significant forces of deformation in our culture today. We have to recognize what these voices are saying and where they are leading us. But that cannot be all. We must also hear and receive what God is telling us. Jesus came to bring better news than anything this world has to offer. We need our minds, our hearts, and our imaginations to be shaped by that good news.

Counter-formation will require us to practice and renew habits of formation—both alone and together. We must study and cultivate historic Christian virtues that have fallen out of favor in the broader culture. We must pursue and prize powerful encounters with God—in all of his truth, goodness, and beauty. By the mercies of God, counter-formation is both possible and worth fighting for together.

How to Use This Counter-Formation Guide

The mission of Frontline Church is multiplying gospel communities that love God, love people, and push back darkness. Our community groups are one of the primary places we live out that mission. This Counter-Formation Guide contains four trainings you can work through together as a community group every two weeks—either in family meals or in discipleship groups. Each session will include a brief Bible discussion, a ten-minute teaching video, discussion questions, and an exercise. The training videos can be accessed at *frontlinechurch.com/formation.*

Most of our community groups follow an "alternating weeks" format, with a family meal on the first and third week of the month, and discipleship groups on the second and fourth week. If your group follows that format, you can work through these trainings in eight weeks (e.g., four consecutive discipleship groups, meeting every other week).

In addition, this Counter-Formation Guide contains 40 daily liturgies for you to work through individually over the course of those same eight weeks. There are five daily liturgies a week, designed to be used as an aid to your time of individual devotion. Each daily liturgy contains a brief call to worship, two Scripture readings, a prayer of confession and assurance, a benediction, and a blank page for notes. The whole process is designed to take no more than fifteen minutes. If you fall behind in any given week, don't feel the need to make up the missed days.

Session 1

What Does It Mean To Be Human?

Session 1

What Does It Mean To Be Human?

Call to Worship

As you begin, have someone pray this prayer out loud for the group. This prayer is based on Psalms 8, 16, and 139.

O LORD, our Lord. Your name is majestic, and your glory endures forever. Who are we that you are mindful of us? God, you are our maker. You have thoughtfully and wonderfully made us. You see us and know us. All your works are perfect. Those who seek you lack no good thing. Today, we seek you, Lord. You are our chosen portion and our cup. Because you have given us yourself, we have a beautiful inheritance. *Amen.*

Bible Conversation

Have someone read the following Scripture and discussion questions out loud. Spend up to 5 minutes in discussion.

Then God said, "Let us make man in our image, after our likeness. And let them have dominion over the fish of the sea and over the birds of the heavens and over the livestock and over all the earth and over every creeping thing that creeps on the earth." So God created man in his own image, in the image of God he created him; male and female he created them. Genesis 1:26-27

- ***In a sentence or two, describe in your own words what you think it means to be human.***

- ***What do you think this Scripture means when it says we are made "in the image of God"?***

Training Notes

Watch the video entitled "What Does It Mean To Be Human?" found at *frontlinechurch.com/formation*. Use the notes below and fill in the blanks to follow along with the video.

What does it mean to be human? This question has haunted humanity since the very beginning. For thousands of years, we have tried to understand who we are and why we exist.

Our Identity as ____________________

Then God said, "Let us make man in our image, after our likeness..." So God created man in his own image, in the image of God he created him; male and female he created them. **Genesis 1:26-27**

Humans were designed to be the image of God in creation. Out of all the things God made, humans were uniquely made to reflect his goodness and greatness.

As the image of God, we are immensely important and valuable—no matter who we are and how we have failed. To be human is to be part of something bigger, something grander than we could possibly imagine.

Our Identity as ____________________

In ancient thought, a king ruled over a kingdom alongside and on behalf of their gods. As the image of a god, a king represented the god he worshipped and ruled with their god's authority.

And God blessed them. And God said to them, "Be fruitful and multiply and fill the earth and subdue it, and have dominion over the fish of the sea and over the birds of the heavens and over every living thing that moves on the earth." **Genesis 1:28**

Humans were designed to rule over creation, under God's authority—to make it good and beautiful just as God intended.

Our Identity as ____________________

The LORD God formed the man of dust from the ground and breathed into his nostrils the breath of life, and the man became a living creature. **Genesis 2:7**

At our core, God made us embodied souls. He could have made us purely spiritual creatures, like the angels. But he made us physical beings with physical bodies. God could have made us purely physical creatures, like the animals. But he made us spiritual beings with immortal souls.

There are no ordinary people. You have never talked to a mere mortal... It is immortals whom we joke with, work with, marry, snub and exploit—immortal horrors or everlasting splendors.
C.S. Lewis, *The Weight of Glory*

Christ has come so human identity can be recovered and cultivated. We can learn again what it means to be human.

Discussion

Have someone read aloud the following description of the Image of God. Then answer the accompanying discussion question.

Scripture teaches that humans are made in the image of God. One of the best ways to understand our role as image bearers is to see ourselves as ambassadors and stewards of God. We could think of ambassadors and stewards of God as those who:

- *take responsibility to promote what is beautiful and fight for what is good*
- *view their speech and conduct as a reflection of God's character*
- *proactively care for what has been entrusted to them—no matter how big or small it might be*
- *give generously and graciously, mirroring their self-giving, gracious God, instead of considering only what people might deserve*
- *make wise decisions in light of eternity instead of reacting foolishly or impulsively*

With those characteristics in mind, answer the following question:

▶ ***If you more fully embraced your identity as an image bearer, what in your life would change for the better?***

Exercise

The following three areas are impacted by your responsibility as an image-bearer of God in the world. Set a timer for five minutes. Each person should silently read through the list and select one area they would most like to grow as an ambassador and steward: work, money, or friendship. Then check one box in that category for a step you would like to take toward growth. After five minutes, whoever is willing can share what they checked and why.

1. Work

- [ ] **Vision.** Name and pursue a God-honoring goal for your work that goes beyond merely earning enough money to meet your needs.
- [ ] **Love.** Aim to tangibly demonstrate love for God and neighbor *at* your work, and *in* your work.

- [ ] ***Diligence.*** Commit to a work ethic marked by excellence and godly ambition. Think of one way to fight the lies of cynicism, impatience, or laziness.

- [ ] ***Rest.*** Make a plan to rest well. Avoid overwork for structural reasons (e.g., the demands of your work) or personal reasons (e.g., the desire for more income).

Learn more by reading *Work That Makes a Difference*, by Dan Doriani

2. Money

- [ ] ***Wisdom.*** Name what season you are in and one way to be faithful within the constraints of that season. Avoid the extremes of being so frugal that you refuse to be generous, on the one hand, and being so lavish that you can't afford to be generous, on the other.

- [ ] ***Sacrifice.*** Love others in such a way that you forgo financial pleasures to meet the needs of others. Name one way you can abstain from your own sense of need in order to give to others.

- [ ] ***Generosity.*** If you prosper, don't automatically assume you should raise your standard of living. Name one area in which you would raise your standard of giving.

- [ ] ***Worship.*** Use money as an act of worship toward Jesus. Name one way you can guard your heart against the love of money, since Jesus warned us we cannot serve two masters (Matt 6:24).

Learn more by reading *Killjoys: The Seven Deadly Sins*, edited by Marshall Segal

3. Friendship

- [ ] ***Presence.*** Pick one way you could better prioritize being together in person with your friends, rather than merely having a digital friendship with others.

- [ ] ***Planning.*** Make friendship a functional priority by setting regular rhythms for connecting over coffee, meals, or other activities. Identify one rhythm to add.

- [ ] ***Affirmation.*** Any time you think of something you respect or admire about a friend, reach out and let them know—right then, on the spot. Every time you get together with a friend, point out one thing that you appreciate about them.

- [ ] ***Depth.*** Model the change you want to see and take conversations one step deeper. Ask good questions. Listen well. Be curious. Then follow up later.

Learn more by reading *Made for Friendship: The Relationship That Halves Our Sorrows and Doubles Our Joys*, by Drew Hunter

Benediction

To conclude your time, pray this prayer out loud together. The following is based on Romans 8:38-39.

For we are sure that neither death nor life, nor angels nor rulers, nor things present nor things to come, nor powers, nor height nor depth, nor anything else in all creation, will be able to separate us from the love of God in Christ Jesus our Lord. *Amen.*

Daily Liturgies: Week 1

Identity and the Image of God

Daily Liturgy: Week 1, Day 1

Identity and the Image of God

Call to Worship

An invitation from God to all humanity to behold and join the story, work, and eternal worship of Jesus. This prayer is based on Psalm 23.

The LORD is my shepherd; I shall not want. My very life is hidden in you. Because of your abundance, I lack nothing. My soul is restless until it finds rest in you. Beside your still waters, I find rest. You, Lord, are a fountain of living water. You overflow with life, and you pour your Spirit into me. Lead me in paths of righteousness for your name's sake. May your goodness and mercy go with me today. *Amen.*

Psalm

A PSALM OF DAVID, WHEN HE FLED FROM ABSALOM HIS SON.

O LORD, how many are my foes!
Many are rising against me;
many are saying of my soul,
"There is no salvation for him in God. SELAH

But you, O LORD, are a shield about me,
my glory, and the lifter of my head.
I cried aloud to the LORD,
and he answered me from his holy hill. SELAH

I lay down and slept;
I woke again, for the LORD sustained me.
I will not be afraid of many thousands of people
who have set themselves against me all around.

Arise, O LORD!
Save me, O my God!
For you strike all my enemies on the cheek;
you break the teeth of the wicked.

Salvation belongs to the LORD;
your blessing be on your people! SELAH

Psalm 3

onfession

A call to acknowledge and forsake sin against God and one another.

Father, my one hope in life and in death is that I am not my own. My body and my soul belong to you. But I have listened to the voice of the world, and let it name me. *Father, forgive me and tune my ears to hear your voice.*

You have given me dignity and worth as your image bearer. But I have listened to the lie that my value comes from status and success. Remind me that the blood of your Son speaks a better word. *Father, forgive me and tune my ears to hear your voice.*

Silently reflect on the ways you have strayed from God's gracious authority. Confess aloud and receive God's free grace through Jesus.

ssurance

An invitation to receive the assurance of a new identity in the finished work of Christ.

Jesus, you did not count equality with God a thing to be grasped, but you humbled yourself, taking the form of a servant. You lived a perfect life under the gaze of God, obeying him without wavering. You died my death, so I might live in your life. You rose again, and you are now seated at the right hand of the Father. You have surely borne my scars, and you will surely bring me home. This is my assurance and my hope. I am fully known by you alone, O Lord. *Thanks be to God!*

ripture Reading

The surrender to God's good and authoritative Word.

In the beginning, God created the heavens and the earth. The earth was without form and void, and darkness was over the face of the deep. And the Spirit of God was hovering over the face of the waters.

And God said, "Let there be light," and there was light. And God saw that the light was good. And God separated the light from the darkness. God called the light Day, and the darkness he called Night. And there was evening and there was morning, the first day.

And God said, "Let there be an expanse in the midst of the waters, and let it separate the waters from the waters." And God made the expanse and separated the waters that were under the expanse from the waters that were above the expanse. And it was so. And God called the expanse Heaven. And there was evening and there was morning, the second day.

And God said, "Let the waters under the heavens be gathered together into one place, and let the dry land appear." And it was so. God called the dry land

Earth, and the waters that were gathered together he called Seas. And God saw that it was good.

And God said, "Let the earth sprout vegetation, plants yielding seed, and fruit trees bearing fruit in which is their seed, each according to its kind, on the earth." And it was so. The earth brought forth vegetation, plants yielding seed according to their own kinds, and trees bearing fruit in which is their seed, each according to its kind. And God saw that it was good. And there was evening and there was morning, the third day.

Genesis 1:1-13

Prayer

An invitation to bring the needs of our bodies, hearts, and minds to the care of God.

Offer prayers for yourself and for others.

Benediction

A blessing from the authority of Scripture spoken over the people of God. The following is based on Philippians 4:7.

May the peace of God, which surpasses all understanding, guard my heart and r mind in Christ Jesus. *Send me now into the world as an image bearer of God.*

Daily Liturgy: Week 1, Day 2

Identity and the Image of God

Call to Worship

An invitation from God to all humanity to behold and join the story, work, and eternal worship of Jesus. This prayer is based on 1 Peter 2.

God, you have made us into a chosen race, a royal priesthood, a holy nation. We are a people of your possession, created to proclaim your excellencies. You have called me out of darkness and into your marvelous light. Once, we were not a people, but now we are your people. Once, I had not received mercy, but now I overflow with your mercy. *Amen.*

Psalm

A SHIGGAION OF DAVID, WHICH HE SANG TO THE LORD CONCERNING THE WORDS OF CUSH, A BENJAMINITE.

O LORD my God, in you do I take refuge;
save me from all my pursuers and deliver me,
lest like a lion they tear my soul apart,
rending it in pieces, with none to deliver.

O LORD my God, if I have done this,
if there is wrong in my hands,
if I have repaid my friend with evil
or plundered my enemy without cause,
let the enemy pursue my soul and overtake it,
and let him trample my life to the ground
and lay my glory in the dust. SELAH

Arise, O LORD, in your anger;
lift yourself up against the fury of my enemies;
awake for me; you have appointed a judgment.
Let the assembly of the peoples be gathered about you;
over it return on high.

Psalm 7:1-7

Confession

A call to acknowledge and forsake sin against God and one another.

Holy God, you made me out of the overflow of your love. I was made to reflect you in my relationship with others, but I have relied on my own strength and walked alone. *Forgive me, O God, for exalting myself above you.*

Holy God, you made me for your glory. I bear your image, and I only come to know myself as I find satisfaction in you. Yet I have looked to others to define me and fulfill me. *Forgive me, O God, for exalting others above you.*

Grant me the courage and humility to move toward others and make much of you.

Silently reflect on the ways you have strayed from God's gracious authority. Confess aloud and receive God's free grace through Jesus.

Assurance

An invitation to receive the assurance of a new identity in the finished work of Christ.

Father, I bring to mind your mercy, and I'm filled with hope. Through the cross and resurrection of Jesus, you brought me home from my wanderings. You've removed my mask, stripped my armor, and clothed me in the righteousness of Christ. You have called me your child, chosen and beloved. Because of you, I am made new and born again to a living hope. Jesus, you are my life, and I am most alive when I make my home in you. *Thanks be to God!*

Scripture Reading

The surrender to God's good and authoritative Word.

And God said, "Let there be lights in the expanse of the heavens to separate the day from the night. And let them be for signs and for seasons, and for days and years, and let them be lights in the expanse of the heavens to give light upon the earth." And it was so. And God made the two great lights—the greater light to rule the day and the lesser light to rule the night—and the stars. And God set them in the expanse of the heavens to give light on the earth, to rule over the day and over the night, and to separate the light from the darkness. And God saw that it was good. And there was evening and there was morning, the fourth day.

And God said, "Let the waters swarm with swarms of living creatures, and let birds fly above the earth across the expanse of the heavens." So God created the great sea creatures and every living creature that moves, with which the waters swarm, according to their kinds, and every winged bird according to its kind. And God saw that it was good. And God blessed them, saying, "Be fruitful and multiply and fill the waters in the seas, and let birds multiply on the earth." And there was evening and there was morning, the fifth day.

And God said, "Let the earth bring forth living creatures according to their kinds—livestock and creeping things and beasts of the earth according to their kinds." And it was so. And God made the beasts of the earth according to their kinds and the livestock according to their kinds, and everything that creeps on the ground according to its kind. And God saw that it was good.

Genesis 1:14-25

Prayer

An invitation to bring the needs of our bodies, hearts, and minds to the care of God.

Offer prayers for yourself and for others.

Benediction

A blessing from the authority of Scripture spoken over the people of God.
The following is based on Revelation 1:5-6.

To him who loves me and has freed me from my sins by his blood and made us a kingdom, priests to his God and Father, to him be glory and dominion forever and ever. *Send me now into the world as an image bearer of God.*

Daily Liturgy: Week 1, Day 3

Identity and the Image of God

Call to Worship

An invitation from God to all humanity to behold and join the story, work, and eternal worship of Jesus. This prayer is based on Colossians 1, Psalm 36, and Psalm 139.

Jesus, you are the image of the invisible God—to see you is to see the Father. All things were created by you, through you, and for you. You made me, knit me together, and called me wonderfully made. Your thoughts toward me are preciou[s] and vast. Your love toward me is rich and unending. I feast at your table and drink from the river of your delights. From you comes life and light. Jesus, you are my life, and I am most alive when I make my home in you. *Amen.*

Psalm

The LORD judges the peoples;
judge me, O LORD, according to my righteousness
and according to the integrity that is in me.
Oh, let the evil of the wicked come to an end,
and may you establish the righteous—
you who test the minds and hearts,
O righteous God!
My shield is with God,
who saves the upright in heart.
God is a righteous judge,
and a God who feels indignation every day.

If a man does not repent, God will whet his sword;
he has bent and readied his bow;
he has prepared for him his deadly weapons,
making his arrows fiery shafts.
Behold, the wicked man conceives evil
and is pregnant with mischief
and gives birth to lies.
He makes a pit, digging it out,
and falls into the hole that he has made.
His mischief returns upon his own head,
and on his own skull his violence descends.
I will give to the LORD the thanks due to his righteousness,
and I will sing praise to the name of the LORD, the Most High.

Psalm 7:8-17

onfession

A call to acknowledge and forsake sin against God and one another.

You are the one who names me. But I confess I have fractured relationship with you by running from your will. Father, your presence is my home. I belong to you and with you. I confess I am often self-centered, self-protective, and self-reliant. *Forgive me and help me return to you.*

I wear my work and reputation as righteousness. I mask myself to fit in. I am a shapeshifter. But I was never meant to bear the weight of creating my own identity. Sin has left my heart fragmented and famished. *Forgive me and help me return to you.*

Silently reflect on the ways you have strayed from God's gracious authority. Confess aloud and receive God's free grace through Jesus.

surance

An invitation to receive the assurance of a new identity in the finished work of Christ.

In Christ, I am a new creation. The old has passed away; the new has come. In Jesus, I am no longer the person I was, or even the person I longed to become. As a beloved and adopted child of God, he invites me to take my place at his table. I am chosen and loved. I have been rescued from every enemy of my soul. Even now, my heart condemns me, but God is greater than my heart. Nothing can separate me from his love. *Thanks be to God!*

ripture Reading

The surrender to God's good and authoritative Word.

Then God said, "Let us make man in our image, after our likeness. And let them have dominion over the fish of the sea and over the birds of the heavens and over the livestock and over all the earth and over every creeping thing that creeps on the earth."

So God created man in his own image,
in the image of God he created him;
male and female he created them.

And God blessed them. And God said to them, "Be fruitful and multiply and fill the earth and subdue it, and have dominion over the fish of the sea and over the birds of the heavens and over every living thing that moves on the earth." And God said, "Behold, I have given you every plant yielding seed that is on the face of all the earth, and every tree with seed in its fruit. You shall have them for food. And to every beast of the earth and to every bird of the heavens and to everything that creeps on the earth, everything that has the breath of life, I have given every green plant for food." And it was so. And God saw everything that he had made, and behold, it was very good. And there was evening and there was morning, the sixth day.

Thus the heavens and the earth were finished, and all the host of them. And on the seventh day God finished his work that he had done, and he rested on the seventh day from all his work that he had done. So God blessed the seventh day and made it holy, because on it God rested from all his work that he had done in creation.

Genesis 1:26 - 2:3

Prayer

An invitation to bring the needs of our bodies, hearts, and minds to the care of God.

Offer prayers for yourself and for others.

Benediction

A blessing from the authority of Scripture spoken over the people of God. The following is based on Romans 11:33, 36.

Oh, the depth of the riches and wisdom and knowledge of God! How unsearchab are his judgments and how inscrutable his ways! For from him and through him and to him are all things. To him be glory forever. *Send me now into the world as an image bearer of God.*

Daily Liturgy: Week 1, Day 4

Identity and the Image of God

Call to Worship

An invitation from God to all humanity to behold and join the story, work, and eternal worship of Jesus. This prayer is based on Psalms 8, 16, and 139.

O LORD, my Lord. Your name is majestic, and your glory endures forever. Who an that you are mindful of me? God, you are my maker. You have thoughtfully and wonderfully made me. You see me and know me. All your works are perfect. Thos who seek you lack no good thing. Today, I seek you, Lord. You are my chosen portion and my cup. Because you have given me yourself, I have a beautiful inheritance. *Amen.*

Psalm

TO THE CHOIRMASTER: ACCORDING TO THE SHEMINITH. A PSALM OF DAVID.

Save, O LORD, for the godly one is gone;
for the faithful have vanished from among the children of man.
Everyone utters lies to his neighbor;
with flattering lips and a double heart they speak.

May the LORD cut off all flattering lips,
the tongue that makes great boasts,
those who say, "With our tongue we will prevail,
our lips are with us; who is master over us?"

"Because the poor are plundered, because the needy groan,
I will now arise," says the LORD;
"I will place him in the safety for which he longs."
The words of the LORD are pure words,
like silver refined in a furnace on the ground,
purified seven times.

You, O LORD, will keep them;
you will guard us from this generation forever.
On every side the wicked prowl,
as vileness is exalted among the children of man.

Psalm 12

Confession

A call to acknowledge and forsake sin against God and one another.

Father, you have made me in your image to reflect your glory. Yet I confess I regularly craft a false image and prefer to seek my own glory. *Forgive me for rejecting who I am in Christ.*

You have asked me to take up my cross, deny myself, and follow you. Yet I confess I often live for myself and follow my sinful desires. *Forgive me for rejecting who I am in Christ.*

You invite me into your peace, promising to lead me, protect me, and provide for me. Yet I confess I often plunge deeper into my anxious thoughts rather than draw near to your presence. *Forgive me for rejecting who I am in Christ.*

Silently reflect on the ways you have strayed from God's gracious authority. Confess aloud and receive God's free grace through Jesus.

Assurance

An invitation to receive the assurance of a new identity in the finished work of Christ.

Father, you promise, for the sake of your Son, to never leave me nor forsake me. I set my hope on your steadfast love. You have started a good work in me, and you are committed to finish it when Jesus returns. *Today, I receive your peace.*

Jesus, you are the Prince of Peace. You died in my place and made peace through the blood of your cross. You made me in your likeness and know me completely. You alone can tell me who I am. *Today, I receive your peace.*

Thanks be to God!

Scripture Reading

The surrender to God's good and authoritative Word.

These are the generations
of the heavens and the earth when they were created,
in the day that the LORD God made the earth and the heavens.

When no bush of the field was yet in the land and no small plant of the field had yet sprung up—for the LORD God had not caused it to rain on the land, and there was no man to work the ground, and a mist was going up from the land and was watering the whole face of the ground— then the LORD God formed the man of dust from the ground and breathed into his nostrils the breath of life, and the man became a living creature. And the LORD God planted a garden in Eden, in the east, and there he put the man whom he had formed. And out of the ground the LORD God made to spring up every tree that is pleasant to the sight and good for food. The tree of life was in the midst of the garden, and the tree of the knowledge of good and evil.

A river flowed out of Eden to water the garden, and there it divided and became four rivers. The name of the first is the Pishon. It is the one that flowed around the whole land of Havilah, where there is gold. And the gold of that land is good; bdellium and onyx stone are there. The name of the second river is the Gihon. It is the one that flowed around the whole land of Cush. And the name of the third river is the Tigris, which flows east of Assyria. And the fourth river is the Euphrates.

The LORD God took the man and put him in the garden of Eden to work it and keep it. And the LORD God commanded the man, saying, "You may surely eat of every tree of the garden, but of the tree of the knowledge of good and evil you shall not eat, for in the day that you eat of it you shall surely die."

Genesis 2:4-17

Prayer

An invitation to bring the needs of our bodies, hearts, and minds to the care of God.

Offer prayers for yourself and for others.

Benediction

A blessing from the authority of Scripture spoken over the people of God.
The following is based on Romans 8:38-39.

For I am sure that neither death nor life, nor angels nor rulers, nor things present nor things to come, nor powers, nor height nor depth, nor anything else in all creation, will be able to separate me from the love of God in Christ Jesus my Lord. *Send me now into the world as an image bearer of God.*

Identity and the Image of God

Call to Worship

An invitation from God to all humanity to behold and join the story, work, and eternal worship of Jesus. This prayer is based on Psalm 23.

The LORD is my shepherd; I shall not want. My very life is hidden in you. Because of your abundance, I lack nothing. My soul is restless until it finds rest in you. Beside your still waters, I find rest. You, Lord, are a fountain of living water. You overflow with life, and you pour your Spirit into me. Lead me in paths of righteousness for your name's sake. May your goodness and mercy go with me today. *Amen.*

Psalm

A PSALM OF DAVID.

O LORD, who shall sojourn in your tent?
Who shall dwell on your holy hill?

He who walks blamelessly and does what is right
and speaks truth in his heart;
who does not slander with his tongue
and does no evil to his neighbor,
nor takes up a reproach against his friend;
in whose eyes a vile person is despised,
but who honors those who fear the LORD;
who swears to his own hurt and does not change;
who does not put out his money at interest
and does not take a bribe against the innocent.
He who does these things shall never be moved.

Psalm 15

Daily Liturgy: Week 1, Day 5

---

onfession

A call to acknowledge and forsake sin against God and one another.

Father, my one hope in life and in death is that I am not my own. My body and my soul belong to you. But I have listened to the voice of the world, and let it name me. *Father, forgive me and tune my ears to hear your voice.*

You have given me dignity and worth as your image bearer. But I have listened to the lie that my value comes from status and success. Remind me that the blood of your Son speaks a better word. *Father, forgive me and tune my ears to hear your voice.*

Silently reflect on the ways you have strayed from God's gracious authority. Confess aloud and receive God's free grace through Jesus.

surance

An invitation to receive the assurance of a new identity in the finished work of Christ.

Jesus, you did not count equality with God a thing to be grasped, but you humbled yourself, taking the form of a servant. You lived a perfect life under the gaze of God, obeying him without wavering. You died my death, so I might live in your life. You rose again, and you are now seated at the right hand of the Father. You have surely borne my scars, and you will surely bring me home. This is my assurance and my hope. I am fully known by you alone, O Lord. *Thanks be to God!*

ripture Reading

The surrender to God's good and authoritative Word.

Then the LORD God said, "It is not good that the man should be alone; I will make him a helper fit for him." Now out of the ground the LORD God had formed every beast of the field and every bird of the heavens and brought them to the man to see what he would call them. And whatever the man called every living creature, that was its name. The man gave names to all livestock and to the birds of the heavens and to every beast of the field. But for Adam there was not found a helper fit for him. So the LORD God caused a deep sleep to fall upon the man, and while he slept took one of his ribs and closed up its place with flesh. And the rib that the LORD God had taken from the man he made into a woman and brought her to the man. Then the man said,

"This at last is bone of my bones
and flesh of my flesh;
she shall be called Woman,
because she was taken out of Man."

Therefore a man shall leave his father and his mother and hold fast to his wife, and they shall become one flesh. And the man and his wife were both naked and were not ashamed.

Genesis 2:18-25

Prayer

An invitation to bring the needs of our bodies, hearts, and minds to the care of God.

Offer prayers for yourself and for others.

Benediction

A blessing from the authority of Scripture spoken over the people of God. The following is based on Philippians 4:7.

May the peace of God, which surpasses all understanding, guard my heart and mind in Christ Jesus. *Send me now into the world as an image bearer of God.*

Daily Liturgies: Week 2

Identity and the Image of God

Daily Liturgy: Week 2, Day 1

Identity and the Image of God

Call to Worship

An invitation from God to all humanity to behold and join the story, work, and eternal worship of Jesus. This prayer is based on 1 Peter 2.

God, you have made us into a chosen race, a royal priesthood, a holy nation. We are a people of your possession, created to proclaim your excellencies. You have called me out of darkness and into your marvelous light. Once, we were not a people, but now we are your people. Once, I had not received mercy, but now I overflow with your mercy. *Amen.*

Psalm

A PRAYER OF DAVID.

Hear a just cause, O LORD; attend to my cry!
Give ear to my prayer from lips free of deceit!
From your presence let my vindication come!
Let your eyes behold the right!

You have tried my heart, you have visited me by night,
you have tested me, and you will find nothing;
I have purposed that my mouth will not transgress.
With regard to the works of man, by the word of your lips
I have avoided the ways of the violent.
My steps have held fast to your paths;
my feet have not slipped.

I call upon you, for you will answer me, O God;
incline your ear to me; hear my words.
Wondrously show your steadfast love,
O Savior of those who seek refuge
from their adversaries at your right hand.

Keep me as the apple of your eye;
hide me in the shadow of your wings,
from the wicked who do me violence,
my deadly enemies who surround me.

They close their hearts to pity;
with their mouths they speak arrogantly.
They have now surrounded our steps;
they set their eyes to cast us to the ground.

He is like a lion eager to tear,
as a young lion lurking in ambush.

Arise, O LORD! Confront him, subdue him!
Deliver my soul from the wicked by your sword,
from men by your hand, O LORD,
from men of the world whose portion is in this life.
You fill their womb with treasure;
they are satisfied with children,
and they leave their abundance to their infants.

As for me, I shall behold your face in righteousness;
when I awake, I shall be satisfied with your likeness.

Psalm 17

Confession

A call to acknowledge and forsake sin against God and one another.

Holy God, you made me out of the overflow of your love. I was made to reflect you in my relationship with others, but I have relied on my own strength and walked alone. *Forgive me, O God, for exalting myself above you.*

Holy God, you made me for your glory. I bear your image, and I only come to know myself as I find satisfaction in you. Yet I have looked to others to define me and fulfill me. *Forgive me, O God, for exalting others above you.*

Grant me the courage and humility to move toward others and make much of you.

Silently reflect on the ways you have strayed from God's gracious authority. Confess aloud and receive God's free grace through Jesus.

Assurance

An invitation to receive the assurance of a new identity in the finished work of Christ.

Father, I bring to mind your mercy, and I'm filled with hope. Through the cross and resurrection of Jesus, you brought me home from my wanderings. You've removed my mask, stripped my armor, and clothed me in the righteousness of Christ. You have called me your child, chosen and beloved. Because of you, I am made new and born again to a living hope. Jesus, you are my life, and I am most alive when I make my home in you. *Thanks be to God!*

Daily Liturgy: Week 2, Day 1

Scripture Reading

The surrender to God's good and authoritative Word.

Now the serpent was more crafty than any other beast of the field that the LORD God had made.

He said to the woman, "Did God actually say, 'You shall not eat of any tree in the garden'?" And the woman said to the serpent, "We may eat of the fruit of the trees in the garden, but God said, You shall not eat of the fruit of the tree that is in the midst of the garden, neither shall you touch it, lest you die.'" But the serpent said to the woman, "You will not surely die. For God knows that when you eat of it your eyes will be opened, and you will be like God, knowing good and evil." So when the woman saw that the tree was good for food, and that it was a delight to the eyes, and that the tree was to be desired to make one wise, she took of its fruit and ate, and she also gave some to her husband who was with her, and he ate. Then the eyes of both were opened, and they knew that they were naked. And they sewed fig leaves together and made themselves loincloths.

And they heard the sound of the LORD God walking in the garden in the cool of the day, and the man and his wife hid themselves from the presence of the LORD God among the trees of the garden. But the LORD God called to the man and said to him, "Where are you?" And he said, "I heard the sound of you in the garden, and I was afraid, because I was naked, and I hid myself." He said, "Who told you that you were naked? Have you eaten of the tree of which I commanded you not to eat?" The man said, "The woman whom you gave to be with me, she gave me fruit of the tree, and I ate." Then the LORD God said to the woman, "What is this that you have done?" The woman said, "The serpent deceived me, and I ate."

Genesis 3:1-13

Prayer

An invitation to bring the needs of our bodies, hearts, and minds to the care of God.

Offer prayers for yourself and for others.

Benediction

A blessing from the authority of Scripture spoken over the people of God.
The following is based on Revelation 1:5-6.

To him who loves me and has freed me from my sins by his blood and made us a kingdom, priests to his God and Father, to him be glory and dominion forever and ever. *Send me now into the world as an image bearer of God.*

Daily Liturgy: Week 2, Day 2

Identity and the Image of God

Call to Worship

An invitation from God to all humanity to behold and join the story, work, and eternal worship of Jesus. This prayer is based on Colossians 1, Psalm 36, and Psalm 139.

Jesus, you are the image of the invisible God—to see you is to see the Father. All things were created by you, through you, and for you. You made me, knit me together, and called me wonderfully made. Your thoughts toward me are precious and vast. Your love toward me is rich and unending. I feast at your table and drink from the river of your delights. From you comes life and light. Jesus, you are my life, and I am most alive when I make my home in you. *Amen.*

Psalm

A PSALM OF DAVID.

The LORD is my shepherd; I shall not want.
He makes me lie down in green pastures.
He leads me beside still waters.
He restores my soul.
He leads me in paths of righteousness
for his name's sake.

Even though I walk through the valley of the shadow of death,
I will fear no evil,
for you are with me;
your rod and your staff,
they comfort me.

You prepare a table before me
in the presence of my enemies;
you anoint my head with oil;
my cup overflows.
Surely goodness and mercy shall follow me
all the days of my life,
and I shall dwell in the house of the LORD forever.

Psalm 23

onfession

A call to acknowledge and forsake sin against God and one another.

You are the one who names me. But I confess I have fractured relationship with you by running from your will. Father, your presence is my home. I belong to you and with you. I confess I am often self-centered, self-protective, and self-reliant. *Forgive me and help me return to you.*

I wear my work and reputation as righteousness. I mask myself to fit in. I am a shapeshifter. But I was never meant to bear the weight of creating my own identity. Sin has left my heart fragmented and famished. *Forgive me and help me return to you.*

Silently reflect on the ways you have strayed from God's gracious authority. Confess aloud and receive God's free grace through Jesus.

surance

An invitation to receive the assurance of a new identity in the finished work of Christ.

In Christ, I am a new creation. The old has passed away; the new has come. In Jesus, I am no longer the person I was, or even the person I longed to become. As a beloved and adopted child of God, he invites me to take my place at his table. I am chosen and loved. I have been rescued from every enemy of my soul. Even now, my heart condemns me, but God is greater than my heart. Nothing can separate me from his love. *Thanks be to God!*

ripture Reading

The surrender to God's good and authoritative Word.

The LORD God said to the serpent,

"Because you have done this,
cursed are you above all livestock
and above all beasts of the field;
on your belly you shall go,
and dust you shall eat
all the days of your life.
I will put enmity between you and the woman,
and between your offspring and her offspring;
he shall bruise your head,
and you shall bruise his heel."

To the woman he said,

Daily Liturgy: Week 2, Day 2

"I will surely multiply your pain in childbearing;
in pain you shall bring forth children.
Your desire shall be contrary to your husband,
but he shall rule over you."

And to Adam he said,

"Because you have listened to the voice of your wife
and have eaten of the tree
of which I commanded you,
'You shall not eat of it,'
cursed is the ground because of you;
in pain you shall eat of it all the days of your life;
thorns and thistles it shall bring forth for you;
and you shall eat the plants of the field.
By the sweat of your face
you shall eat bread,
till you return to the ground,
for out of it you were taken;
for you are dust,
and to dust you shall return."

The man called his wife's name Eve, because she was the mother of all living. And the LORD God made for Adam and for his wife garments of skins and clothed them.

Then the LORD God said, "Behold, the man has become like one of us in knowing good and evil. Now, lest he reach out his hand and take also of the tree of life and eat, and live forever—" therefore the LORD God sent him out from the garden of Eden to work the ground from which he was taken. He drove out the man, and at the east of the garden of Eden he placed the cherubim and a flaming sword that turned every way to guard the way to the tree of life.

Genesis 3:14-24

Prayer

An invitation to bring the needs of our bodies, hearts, and minds to the care of God.

Offer prayers for yourself and for others.

Benediction

A blessing from the authority of Scripture spoken over the people of God. The following is based on Romans 11:33, 36.

Oh, the depth of the riches and wisdom and knowledge of God! How unsearchable are his judgments and how inscrutable his ways! For from him and through him and to him are all things. To him be glory forever. *Send me now into the world as an image bearer of God.*

Daily Liturgy: Week 2, Day 3

Identity and the Image of God

Call to Worship

An invitation from God to all humanity to behold and join the story, work, and eternal worship of Jesus. This prayer is based on Psalms 8, 16, and 139.

O LORD, my Lord. Your name is majestic, and your glory endures forever. Who am I that you are mindful of me? God, you are my maker. You have thoughtfully and wonderfully made me. You see me and know me. All your works are perfect. Those who seek you lack no good thing. Today, I seek you, Lord. You are my chosen portion and my cup. Because you have given me yourself, I have a beautiful inheritance. *Amen.*

Psalm

OF DAVID.

Vindicate me, O LORD,
for I have walked in my integrity,
and I have trusted in the LORD without wavering.
Prove me, O LORD, and try me;
test my heart and my mind.
For your steadfast love is before my eyes,
and I walk in your faithfulness.

I do not sit with men of falsehood,
nor do I consort with hypocrites.
I hate the assembly of evildoers,
and I will not sit with the wicked.

I wash my hands in innocence
and go around your altar, O LORD,
proclaiming thanksgiving aloud,
and telling all your wondrous deeds.

O LORD, I love the habitation of your house
and the place where your glory dwells.
Do not sweep my soul away with sinners,
nor my life with bloodthirsty men,
in whose hands are evil devices,
and whose right hands are full of bribes.

But as for me, I shall walk in my integrity;
redeem me, and be gracious to me.

My foot stands on level ground;
in the great assembly I will bless the LORD.

Psalm 26

nfession

A call to acknowledge and forsake sin against God and one another.

Father, you have made me in your image to reflect your glory. Yet I confess I regularly craft a false image and prefer to seek my own glory. *Forgive me for rejecting who I am in Christ.*

You have asked me to take up my cross, deny myself, and follow you. Yet I confess I often live for myself and follow my sinful desires. *Forgive me for rejecting who I am in Christ.*

You invite me into your peace, promising to lead me, protect me, and provide for me. Yet I confess I often plunge deeper into my anxious thoughts rather than draw near to your presence. *Forgive me for rejecting who I am in Christ.*

Silently reflect on the ways you have strayed from God's gracious authority. Confess aloud and receive God's free grace through Jesus.

surance

An invitation to receive the assurance of a new identity in the finished work of Christ.

Father, you promise, for the sake of your Son, to never leave me nor forsake me. I set my hope on your steadfast love. You have started a good work in me, and you are committed to finish it when Jesus returns. *Today, I receive your peace.*

Jesus, you are the Prince of Peace. You died in my place and made peace through the blood of your cross. You made me in your likeness and know me completely. You alone can tell me who I am. *Today, I receive your peace.*

Thanks be to God!

ripture Reading

The surrender to God's good and authoritative Word.

Now Adam knew Eve his wife, and she conceived and bore Cain, saying, "I have gotten a man with the help of the LORD." And again, she bore his brother Abel. Now Abel was a keeper of sheep, and Cain a worker of the ground. In the course of time Cain brought to the LORD an offering of the fruit of the ground, and Abel also brought of the firstborn of his flock and of their fat portions. And the LORD had regard for Abel and his offering, but for Cain and his offering he had no regard. So Cain was very angry, and his face fell. The LORD said to Cain, "Why ar you angry, and why has your face fallen? If you do well, will you not be accepted? And if you do not do well, sin is crouching at the door. Its desire is contrary to you but you must rule over it."

Cain spoke to Abel his brother. And when they were in the field, Cain rose up against his brother Abel and killed him. Then the LORD said to Cain, "Where is Abel your brother?" He said, "I do not know; am I my brother's keeper?" And the LORD said, "What have you done? The voice of your brother's blood is crying to me from the ground. And now you are cursed from the ground, which has opened its mouth to receive your brother's blood from your hand. When you work the ground, it shall no longer yield to you its strength. You shall be a fugitive and a wanderer on the earth." Cain said to the LORD, "My punishment is greater than I can bear. Behold, you have driven me today away from the ground, and from your face I shall be hidden. I shall be a fugitive and a wanderer on the earth and whoever finds me will kill me." Then the LORD said to him, "Not so! If anyone kills Cain, vengeance shall be taken on him sevenfold." And the LORD put a mark on Cain, lest any who found him should attack him. Then Cain went away from the presence of the LORD and settled in the land of Nod, east of Eden.

Genesis 4:1-16

Prayer

An invitation to bring the needs of our bodies, hearts, and minds to the care of God.

Offer prayers for yourself and for others.

Benediction

A blessing from the authority of Scripture spoken over the people of God.
The following is based on Romans 8:38-39.

For I am sure that neither death nor life, nor angels nor rulers, nor things presen nor things to come, nor powers, nor height nor depth, nor anything else in all creation, will be able to separate me from the love of God in Christ Jesus my Lor
Send me now into the world as an image bearer of God.

Daily Liturgy: Week 2, Day 4

Identity and the Image of God

Call to Worship

An invitation from God to all humanity to behold and join the story, work, and eternal worship of Jesus. This prayer is based on Psalm 23.

The LORD is my shepherd; I shall not want. My very life is hidden in you. Because of your abundance, I lack nothing. My soul is restless until it finds rest in you. Beside your still waters, I find rest. You, Lord, are a fountain of living water. You overflow with life, and you pour your Spirit into me. Lead me in paths of righteousness for your name's sake. May your goodness and mercy go with me today. *Amen.*

Psalm

A MASKIL OF DAVID.

Blessed is the one whose transgression is forgiven,
whose sin is covered.
Blessed is the man against whom the LORD counts no iniquity,
and in whose spirit there is no deceit.

For when I kept silent, my bones wasted away
through my groaning all day long.
For day and night your hand was heavy upon me;
my strength was dried up as by the heat of summer. SELAH

I acknowledged my sin to you,
and I did not cover my iniquity;
I said, "I will confess my transgressions to the LORD,"
and you forgave the iniquity of my sin. SELAH

Therefore let everyone who is godly
offer prayer to you at a time when you may be found;
surely in the rush of great waters,
they shall not reach him.
You are a hiding place for me;
you preserve me from trouble;
you surround me with shouts of deliverance. SELAH

I will instruct you and teach you in the way you should go;
I will counsel you with my eye upon you.
Be not like a horse or a mule, without understanding,
which must be curbed with bit and bridle,
or it will not stay near you.

Many are the sorrows of the wicked,
but steadfast love surrounds the one who trusts in the LORD.
Be glad in the LORD, and rejoice, O righteous,
and shout for joy, all you upright in heart!

Psalm 32

Confession

A call to acknowledge and forsake sin against God and one another.

Father, my one hope in life and in death is that I am not my own. My body and my soul belong to you. But I have listened to the voice of the World, and let it name me. *Father, forgive me and tune my ears to hear your voice.*

You have given me dignity and worth as your image bearer. But I have listened to the lie that my value comes from status and success. Remind me that the blood of your Son speaks a better word. *Father, forgive me and tune my ears to hear your voice.*

Silently reflect on the ways you have strayed from God's gracious authority. Confess aloud and receive God's free grace through Jesus.

Assurance

An invitation to receive the assurance of a new identity in the finished work of Christ.

Jesus, you did not count equality with God a thing to be grasped, but you humbled yourself, taking the form of a servant. You lived a perfect life under the gaze of God, obeying him without wavering. You died my death, so I might live in your life. You rose again, and you are now seated at the right hand of the Father. You have surely borne my scars, and you will surely bring me home. This is my assurance and my hope. I am fully known by you alone, O Lord. *Thanks be to God!*

Scripture Reading

The surrender to God's good and authoritative Word.

Cain knew his wife, and she conceived and bore Enoch. When he built a city, he called the name of the city after the name of his son, Enoch. To Enoch was born Irad, and Irad fathered Mehujael, and Mehujael fathered Methushael, and Methushael fathered Lamech. And Lamech took two wives. The name of the one was Adah, and the name of the other Zillah. Adah bore Jabal; he was the father of those who dwell in tents and have livestock. His brother's name was Jubal; he was the father of all those who play the lyre and pipe. Zillah also bore Tubal-cain; he was the forger of all instruments of bronze and iron. The sister of Tubal-cain was Naamah.

Lamech said to his wives:

"Adah and Zillah, hear my voice;
you wives of Lamech, listen to what I say:
I have killed a man for wounding me,
a young man for striking me.
If Cain's revenge is sevenfold,
then Lamech's is seventy-sevenfold."

And Adam knew his wife again, and she bore a son and called his name Seth, for she said, "God has appointed for me another offspring instead of Abel, for Cain killed him." To Seth also a son was born, and he called his name Enosh. At that time people began to call upon the name of the LORD.

Genesis 4:17-26

Prayer

An invitation to bring the needs of our bodies, hearts, and minds to the care of God.

Offer prayers for yourself and for others.

Benediction

A blessing from the authority of Scripture spoken over the people of God.
The following is based on Philippians 4:7.

May the peace of God, which surpasses all understanding, guard my heart and my mind in Christ Jesus. *Send me now into the world as an image bearer of God.*

Daily Liturgy: Week 2, Day 5

Identity and the Image of God

Call to Worship

An invitation from God to all humanity to behold and join the story, work, and eternal worship of Jesus. This prayer is based on 1 Peter 2.

God, you have made us into a chosen race, a royal priesthood, a holy nation. We are a people of your possession, created to proclaim your excellencies. You have called me out of darkness and into your marvelous light. Once, we were not a people, but now we are your people. Once, I had not received mercy, but now I overflow with your mercy. *Amen.*

Psalm

TO THE CHOIRMASTER. OF DAVID, THE SERVANT OF THE LORD.

Transgression speaks to the wicked
deep in his heart;
there is no fear of God
before his eyes.
For he flatters himself in his own eyes
that his iniquity cannot be found out and hated.
The words of his mouth are trouble and deceit;
he has ceased to act wisely and do good.
He plots trouble while on his bed;
he sets himself in a way that is not good;
he does not reject evil.

Your steadfast love, O LORD, extends to the heavens,
your faithfulness to the clouds.
Your righteousness is like the mountains of God;
your judgments are like the great deep;
man and beast you save, O LORD.

How precious is your steadfast love, O God!
The children of mankind take refuge in the shadow of your wings.
They feast on the abundance of your house,
and you give them drink from the river of your delights.
For with you is the fountain of life;
in your light do we see light.

Oh, continue your steadfast love to those who know you,
and your righteousness to the upright of heart!
Let not the foot of arrogance come upon me,
nor the hand of the wicked drive me away.

There the evildoers lie fallen;
they are thrust down, unable to rise.

Psalm 36

Confession

A call to acknowledge and forsake sin against God and one another.

Holy God, you made me out of the overflow of your love. I was made to reflect you in my relationship with others, but I have relied on my own strength and walked alone. *Forgive me, O God, for exalting myself above you.*

Holy God, you made me for your glory. I bear your image, and I only come to know myself as I find satisfaction in you. Yet I have looked to others to define me and fulfill me. *Forgive me, O God, for exalting others above you.*

Grant me the courage and humility to move toward others and make much of you.

Silently reflect on the ways you have strayed from God's gracious authority. Confess aloud and receive God's free grace through Jesus.

Assurance

An invitation to receive the assurance of a new identity in the finished work of Christ.

Father, I bring to mind your mercy, and I'm filled with hope. Through the cross and resurrection of Jesus, you brought me home from my wanderings. You've removed my mask, stripped my armor, and clothed me in the righteousness of Christ. You have called me your child, chosen and beloved. Because of you, I am made new and born again to a living hope. Jesus, you are my life, and I am most alive when I make my home in you. *Thanks be to God!*

Scripture Reading

The surrender to God's good and authoritative Word.

This is the book of the generations of Adam. When God created man, he made him in the likeness of God. Male and female he created them, and he blessed them and named them Man when they were created. When Adam had lived 130 years, he fathered a son in his own likeness, after his image, and named him Seth. The days of Adam after he fathered Seth were 800 years; and he had other sons and daughters. Thus all the days that Adam lived were 930 years, and he died.

Daily Liturgy: Week 2, Day 5

When Seth had lived 105 years, he fathered Enosh. Seth lived after he fathered Enosh 807 years and had other sons and daughters. Thus all the days of Seth wer 912 years, and he died.

When Enosh had lived 90 years, he fathered Kenan. Enosh lived after he fathered Kenan 815 years and had other sons and daughters. Thus all the days of Enosh were 905 years, and he died.

When Kenan had lived 70 years, he fathered Mahalalel. Kenan lived after he fathered Mahalalel 840 years and had other sons and daughters. Thus all the day of Kenan were 910 years, and he died.

When Mahalalel had lived 65 years, he fathered Jared. Mahalalel lived after he fathered Jared 830 years and had other sons and daughters. Thus all the days of Mahalalel were 895 years, and he died.

When Jared had lived 162 years, he fathered Enoch. Jared lived after he fathered Enoch 800 years and had other sons and daughters. Thus all the days of Jared were 962 years, and he died.

When Enoch had lived 65 years, he fathered Methuselah. Enoch walked with God after he fathered Methuselah 300 years and had other sons and daughters. Thus all the days of Enoch were 365 years. Enoch walked with God, and he was not, fo God took him.

When Methuselah had lived 187 years, he fathered Lamech. Methuselah lived after he fathered Lamech 782 years and had other sons and daughters. Thus all the days of Methuselah were 969 years, and he died.

When Lamech had lived 182 years, he fathered a son and called his name Noah, saying, "Out of the ground that the LORD has cursed, this one shall bring us relie from our work and from the painful toil of our hands." Lamech lived after he fathered Noah 595 years and had other sons and daughters. Thus all the days of Lamech were 777 years, and he died.

After Noah was 500 years old, Noah fathered Shem, Ham, and Japheth.

Genesis 5:1-32

Prayer

An invitation to bring the needs of our bodies, hearts, and minds to the care of God.

Offer prayers for yourself and for others.

Benediction

A blessing from the authority of Scripture spoken over the people of God. The following is based on Revelation 1:5-6.

To him who loves me and has freed me from my sins by his blood and made us a kingdom, priests to his God and Father, to him be glory and dominion forever and ever. *Send me now into the world as an image bearer of God.*

Session 2

What Does It Mean To Be Me?

Session 2

What Does It Mean To Be Me?

Call to Worship

As you begin, have someone pray this prayer out loud for the group. This prayer is based on Psalm 23.

The LORD is our shepherd; we shall not want. Our very lives are hidden in you. Because of your abundance, we lack nothing. Our souls are restless until they find rest in you. Beside your still waters, we find rest. You, Lord, are a fountain of living water. You overflow with life, and you pour your Spirit into us. Lead us in paths of righteousness for your name's sake. May your goodness and mercy go with us today. *Amen.*

Bible Conversation

Have someone read the following Scripture and discussion question out loud. Spend up to 5 minutes in discussion.

O LORD, you have searched me and known me! You know when I sit down and when I rise up; you discern my thoughts from afar. You search out my path and my lying down and are acquainted with all my ways... For you formed my inward parts; you knitted me together in my mother's womb. I praise you, for I am fearfully and wonderfully made. Wonderful are your works; my soul knows it very well. **Psalm 139:1-3, 13-14**

▶ ***How does God's intimate knowledge of you change the way you think about your identity? How should it impact the way you live?***

Training Notes

Watch the video entitled "What Does It Mean To Be Me?" found at *frontlinechurch.com/formation*. Use the notes below and fill in the blanks to follow along with the video.

I didn't have a secret life. But I had a secret dream life—which might have been worse. I loved my husband; it's not that I didn't. But I felt that he was standing between me and the world, between me and myself. Everything I experienced—relationships, reality, my understanding of my own identity and desires—were filtered through him before I could access them... It was like I was always on my tiptoes, trying to see around him. I couldn't see, but I could imagine. I started imagining other lives. Other homes... It was as if everything looked different. Not better or worse, just clearer, harsher... I had caused so much upheaval, so much suffering, and for what?... So I could put my face in the wind. So I could see the sun's glare.
Honor Jones, "How I Demolished My Life"

Who are we, really? What is the essence of our personal identity? Why is it so hard to know the "real me"?

Knowing Our creator

If we are indeed uniquely made by God, he himself ought to know who we are and why we exist. He knows every part of us and the reason he made us.

> *O LORD, you have searched me and known me! You know when I sit down and when I rise up; you discern my thoughts from afar. You search out my path and my lying down and are acquainted with all my ways... For you formed my inward parts; you knitted me together in my mother's womb. I praise you, for I am fearfully and wonderfully made. Wonderful are your works; my soul knows it very well.* **Psalm 139:1-3, 13-14**

If we want to find our true identity, we have to look for it, not in ourselves, but in God's words to us. In fact, because of sin, our ability to understand ourselves is massively impaired.

> *One may understand the cosmos, but never the ego; the self is more distant than any star. Thou shalt love the Lord thy God; but thou shalt not know thyself. We are all under the same mental calamity; we have all forgotten our names. We have all forgotten what we really are.* **G. K. Chesterton, *Orthodoxy***

If we want to know ourselves more fully, we have to grow in knowing the One who made us.

Knowing Our Story

> *It's like everyone tells a story about themselves inside their own head. Always. All the time. That story makes you what you are. We build ourselves out of that story.* **Patrick Rothfuss, *The Name of the Wind***

We all have a story. We all come from somewhere. Each one of us have experienced moments and relationships that have influenced who we are today.

Each culture tends to elevate certain identity markers over others. As a result, we often feel pressure to put our eggs in one or two baskets, which sets us up for identity crisis when our world comes crashing down.

> *While some markers are more set than others, many can change over time. If I look to my possessions or occupation for my identity, for example, what happens if I suffer a financial setback, lose my job, or retire? If my marital*

status is the main feature of who I am, what happens if that changes? It is a mistake to reduce any human being's identity to one immutable marker. We are more complicated than that. **Brian Rosner, *How To Find Yourself***

Scripture encourages us that, while our story is significant, it isn't ultimate. We should work toward understanding our story better, but always in light of the story God is telling.

Knowing Our heart

The biblical picture of the heart is much broader than we often think.

The heart includes what we know (our knowledge, thoughts, intentions, ideas, meditation, memory, imagination), what we love (what we want, seek, feel, yearn for), and what we choose (whether we will resist or submit, whether we will be weak or strong, whether we will say yes or no). **A. Craig Troxel, *With All Your Heart***

We are whole persons and cannot be reduced to "feeling" creatures only. The complexities of our inner life speak to what makes us who we truly are. In this sense, the heart is vital to our sense of self, to our identity.

You have made us for yourself, O Lord, and our heart is restless until it rests in you. **Augustine, *Confessions***

This doesn't mean we should wholesale disregard our hearts, nor follow them with abandon. Rather, we should listen to our hearts with caution. And when our hearts go astray, we should direct our hearts back to God.

Discussion

Have someone read aloud the following adaptation from *How To Find Yourself* by Brian Rosner. Then answer the accompanying discussion question.

People today increasingly have what sociologists call the "buffered self," a self defined and shaped from within, to the exclusion of external roles and ties. We find our true selves by detaching ourselves from external influences like home, family, religion, and tradition, and thereby determine who we are for ourselves.. Self-definition is thus the culturally endorsed route to identity-formation in our day. Today we have a do-it-yourself self or a self-made self, which looks only inward to find itself. Academics call this *expressive individualism*.

Expressive individualism is marked by the following characteristics:

1. **The best way to find yourself is to look inward.**
2. **The highest goal in life is happiness.**
3. **All moral judgments are merely expressions of feeling or personal preference.**

4. Forms of external authority are to be rejected.
5. The world will improve dramatically as the scope of individual freedom grows.
6. Everyone's quest for self-expression should be celebrated.
7. Certain aspects of a person's identity—such as their gender, ethnicity, or sexuality—are of paramount importance.

▶ ***Looking back over your life, which one of these characteristics of "expressive individualism" has most influenced your understanding of identity? Do any of the characteristics ring true for you, and if so, how strongly do you feel about them?***

Exercise

In order to know our hearts better, it is important to grow in our awareness of our own sins, wounds, and weaknesses. Self-awareness is an important part of spiritual maturity. Set a timer for five minutes. Each person should silently work through the following assessment adapted from *The Emotionally Healthy Leader*, by Peter Scazzaro. Then answer the accompanying question.

Next to each statement, write down the number that best describes your response. Use the following scale:

5 — *Always* true of me
4 — *Frequently* true of me
3 — *Occasionally* true of me
2 — *Rarely* true of me
1 — *Never* true of me

____ I take time regularly to admit and speak aloud my anger, fear, and sadness to God and others.

____ I have a healthy awareness of my wounds, self-protectiveness, and weaknesses—and how I am tempted to sin against other people in my unguarded moments.

____ When I overreact, rather than blaming others, I settle myself down and ask, "What from my past might be tempting me to react so strongly to this situation or person?"

____ I am honest with myself and a few significant others about the sins, struggles, doubts, and hurts deep beneath the surface of my life.

____ I routinely seek out and embrace feedback from other people about how they experience my flaws.

____ I take the time to ask hard questions of myself even when I am fearful of where the answers might lead.

____ I consistently seek out guidance from my spiritual leaders, other mentors, a counselor, a spiritual director, or other mature believers to help me process how my sins, wounds, and weaknesses manifests themselves in my life.

2 I quickly reach out for help when I notice tension in my mind or in my body, or find myself engaging in unhealthy or self-destructive behaviors.

5 I am able to identify the connections between my weaknesses and sins (mixed motives, fear of man, anxiety, anger, etc.) and my family of origin or my personal story.

4 I am able to anticipate moments and seasons that might be difficult for me and to ask for support in advance.

After the five minutes, answer the following question.

- ***What was the experience of filling out that assessment like for you personally? What encouraged you? Discouraged you? Surprised you?***

Benediction

To conclude your time, pray this prayer out loud together. The following is based on Philippians 4:7.

May the peace of God, which surpasses all understanding, guard our hearts and our minds in Christ Jesus. *Amen.*

Why Self-Analysis Cannot Save Us

A Take-Home Resource

Are we encouraging you to go on an inward hunt for "the idols" in your hearts? Are we encouraging you to hunt for "the idols" in someone else's heart? Is figuring out what is wrong *the* key to changing? Should we be continually looking in the mirror? No—not at all! Here is a helpful "take-home" excerpt from an article by Davi Powlison entitled "Revisiting Idols of the Heart and Vanity Fair" (*Journal of Biblical Counseling* 27:3, 2013).

[Am I calling you] to obsessively introspective self-analysis? Never. [Am I invitin you] to nosy mind-reading of others' motives? Never. Self-analysis cannot save u It can become simply one more form of self-fascination. Other-analysis cannot save others. It can become simply one more form of judgmentalism.

True self-knowledge is a fine gift. And true self-knowledge always leads us out o ourselves, and to our Father who, knowing us thoroughly, loves us utterly. True self-knowledge does not wallow around inside. God intends to draw us out of se preoccupation. Seeing the vertical dimension of the struggle with sin and death, we reach out more boldly to the One who is life and light. There are many reasor not to go on an idol-hunt. Here are [two] of those reasons.

First, our renegade desires are not so complicated as to necessitate a "hunt."

The desires that mislead us are self-deceiving, because we are so plausible to ourselves. And lies whispering inside our heads can be hard to identify—but th are not as complicated as we might imagine. For example, whenever I complain, grumble or criticize, these sins are wedded to straightforward motives.
I grumble because

I *want* ________.

I *fear* ________.

I *need* ________.

I *expect* ________.

Fill in the blanks and you've named the nasty God-substitute that fires up a bad attitude. I am mastered by MY kingdom come and MY will be done. I erase God from his universe—unbelief. I exalt myself—pride. I am enslaved to what I most want—lust. So the sins of grumbling have an identifiable "psychological" dimension. They also have a "sociological" dimension. When I grumble, I confor to the community of grumblers and want things that current opinion, cultural values, and modern advertising teach me to need. And the sins of grumbling als have a "Satan-like" dimension. I am exhibiting what James 3:14–16 portrays as th logic of a devilish wisdom.

It is helpful to name the mastering lust, fear, felt-need or expectation that hijacks God's place. Repentance becomes more intelligent. I can bring to the Father of mercies both my visible behavior and my inner motives. His love is magnified because I see my need for mercy more clearly. *For your name's sake pardon my iniquity, for it is very great* (Ps 25:11). And he freely, willingly forgives his beloved children. When he thinks about me and about you, he remembers his own loving kindness, and he answers our plea.

[Second], our renegade desires are not so "deep" as to call for intense introspection.

The desires that mislead us do cause us to coil in on ourselves, but that doesn't mean that the content of our mastering desires hides deep within some inner labyrinth. They are not as inward as we might imagine. In fact, they are not really "intra-psychological" phenomena at all. Our motives are all active verbs that describe how we connect to the world around us: What are you seeking? What are you loving? What are you fearing? What are you trusting? Where are you taking refuge? What voices are you listening to? Where are you setting your hopes? The answers to these questions describe characteristics of the whole person, who always orients toward either God or something else. They always propel us to view and treat other people either wisely or foolishly—so they are closely linked to actual behavior, emotions, and attitudes. When we take the Bible's God-relational verbs and turn them into questions, we are exposed for what we are. Such questions can help you to see how and why you are straying. They can help you help others to see themselves. Our answers to these questions describe the seedbed of our sins, how we curve in on ourselves and go blind to God and his will.

But such questions never intend to send you spiraling down on an inward journey. They don't intend to make you intrusively probe others for hidden dirt. They do invite all of us to come out of the dark and into the light of Christ. Seek him who is worthy. Trust him who gives freely. Love him who is lovely. Fear him before whom we stand. Take refuge in the one who truly is our shelter.

I think that "idols of the heart" is a great metaphor (if we don't overuse it!). It captures the match between inward desire and outward objects of desire. People are always reaching out to worship something, anything—either God or the mini-gods. Sin causes the psyche to operate as if we were self-referential and encapsulated. But our souls are in fact God-relational and God-accountable. The sense of self-encapsulation with which we experience our desires simply describes our defection from reality.

I'll risk redundancy because this issue is so important. If I go on an "idol-hunt" into myself, I become intensely introspective and self-analytical. Similarly, if I go on an "idol-hunt" into you, I try to read your mind, as if I could peer into your heart, as if I had the right to judge you. Idol-hunts of any kind forget that knowing ourselves and others is not an end in itself. Accurate knowledge of our need leads directly away from ourselves and into the mercies of God for us and for others.

Faith makes self-knowledge look to God and relate to him. Faith is not introspective.

Love makes knowledge of others generous-hearted and merciful. Love is not judgmental.

Faith and love draw us out of sin's enmeshing self-obsession (including enmeshment in obsessive introspection). So come forth. Our Savior gives us his own joy, and joy is an interpersonal emotion. He throws open the doors to the fresh air and bright light of a most kind grace. Bless the Lord, O my soul, and all that is within me bless his holy name!

Daily Liturgies: Week 3

Identity and the Self

Daily Liturgy: Week 3, Day 1

Identity and the Self

Call to Worship

An invitation from God to all humanity to behold and join the story, work, and eterna worship of Jesus. This prayer is based on Colossians 1, Psalm 36, and Psalm 139.

Jesus, you are the image of the invisible God—to see you is to see the Father. All things were created by you, through you, and for you. You made me, knit me together, and called me wonderfully made. Your thoughts toward me are precio and vast. Your love toward me is rich and unending. I feast at your table and drin from the river of your delights. From you comes life and light. Jesus, you are my life, and I am most alive when I make my home in you. *Amen.*

Psalm

TO THE CHOIRMASTER. A PSALM OF DAVID.

Blessed is the one who considers the poor!
In the day of trouble the LORD delivers him;
the LORD protects him and keeps him alive;
he is called blessed in the land;
you do not give him up to the will of his enemies.
The LORD sustains him on his sickbed;
in his illness you restore him to full health.

As for me, I said, "O LORD, be gracious to me;
heal me, for I have sinned against you!"
My enemies say of me in malice,
"When will he die, and his name perish?"
And when one comes to see me, he utters empty words,
while his heart gathers iniquity;
when he goes out, he tells it abroad.
All who hate me whisper together about me;
they imagine the worst for me.

They say, "A deadly thing is poured out on him;
he will not rise again from where he lies."
Even my close friend in whom I trusted,
who ate my bread, has lifted his heel against me.
But you, O LORD, be gracious to me,
and raise me up, that I may repay them!

By this I know that you delight in me:
my enemy will not shout in triumph over me.
But you have upheld me because of my integrity,
and set me in your presence forever.

Blessed be the LORD, the God of Israel,
from everlasting to everlasting!
Amen and Amen.

Psalm 41

Confession

A call to acknowledge and forsake sin against God and one another.

You are the one who names me. But I confess I have fractured relationship with you by running from your will. Father, your presence is my home. I belong to you and with you. I confess I am often self-centered, self-protective, and self-reliant. *Forgive me and help me return to you.*

I wear my work and reputation as righteousness. I mask myself to fit in. I am a shapeshifter. But I was never meant to bear the weight of creating my own identity. Sin has left my heart fragmented and famished. *Forgive me and help me return to you.*

Silently reflect on the ways you have strayed from God's gracious authority. Confess aloud and receive God's free grace through Jesus.

ssurance

An invitation to receive the assurance of a new identity in the finished work of Christ.

In Christ, I am a new creation. The old has passed away; the new has come. In Jesus, I am no longer the person I was, or even the person I longed to become. As a beloved and adopted child of God, he invites me to take my place at his table. I am chosen and loved. I have been rescued from every enemy of my soul. Even now, my heart condemns me, but God is greater than my heart. Nothing can separate me from his love. *Thanks be to God!*

:ripture Reading

The surrender to God's good and authoritative Word.

When man began to multiply on the face of the land and daughters were born to them, the sons of God saw that the daughters of man were attractive. And they took as their wives any they chose. Then the LORD said, "My Spirit shall not abide in man forever, for he is flesh: his days shall be 120 years." The Nephilim were on the earth in those days, and also afterward, when the sons of God came in to the daughters of man and they bore children to them. These were the mighty men who were of old, the men of renown.

Daily Liturgy: Week 3, Day 1

The LORD saw that the wickedness of man was great in the earth, and that every intention of the thoughts of his heart was only evil continually. And the LORD regretted that he had made man on the earth, and it grieved him to his heart. So the LORD said, "I will blot out man whom I have created from the face of the land, man and animals and creeping things and birds of the heavens, for I am sorry that I have made them." But Noah found favor in the eyes of the LORD.

Genesis 6:1-8

Prayer

An invitation to bring the needs of our bodies, hearts, and minds to the care of God.

Offer prayers for yourself and for others.

Benediction

A blessing from the authority of Scripture spoken over the people of God.
The following is based on Romans 11:33, 36.

Oh, the depth of the riches and wisdom and knowledge of God! How unsearchable are his judgments and how inscrutable his ways! For from him and through him and to him are all things. To him be glory forever. *Send me now into the world as an image bearer of God.*

Daily Liturgy: Week 3, Day 2

Identity and the Self

Call to Worship

An invitation from God to all humanity to behold and join the story, work, and eternal worship of Jesus. This prayer is based on Psalms 8, 16, and 139.

O LORD, my Lord. Your name is majestic, and your glory endures forever. Who am I that you are mindful of me? God, you are my maker. You have thoughtfully and wonderfully made me. You see me and know me. All your works are perfect. Those who seek you lack no good thing. Today, I seek you, Lord. You are my chosen portion and my cup. Because you have given me yourself, I have a beautiful inheritance. *Amen.*

Psalm

TO THE CHOIRMASTER: A PSALM OF THE SONS OF KORAH.

Clap your hands, all peoples!
Shout to God with loud songs of joy!
For the LORD, the Most High, is to be feared,
a great king over all the earth.
He subdued peoples under us,
and nations under our feet.
He chose our heritage for us,
the pride of Jacob whom he loves. SELAH

God has gone up with a shout,
the LORD with the sound of a trumpet.
Sing praises to God, sing praises!
Sing praises to our King, sing praises!
For God is the King of all the earth;
sing praises with a psalm!

God reigns over the nations;
God sits on his holy throne.
The princes of the peoples gather
as the people of the God of Abraham.
For the shields of the earth belong to God;
he is highly exalted!

Psalm 47

nfession

A call to acknowledge and forsake sin against God and one another.

Father, you have made me in your image to reflect your glory. Yet I confess I regularly craft a false image and prefer to seek my own glory. *Forgive me for rejecting who I am in Christ.*

You have asked me to take up my cross, deny myself, and follow you. Yet I confess I often live for myself and follow my sinful desires. *Forgive me for rejecting who I am in Christ.*

You invite me into your peace, promising to lead me, protect me, and provide for me. Yet I confess I often plunge deeper into my anxious thoughts rather than draw near to your presence. *Forgive me for rejecting who I am in Christ.*

Silently reflect on the ways you have strayed from God's gracious authority. Confess aloud and receive God's free grace through Jesus.

surance

An invitation to receive the assurance of a new identity in the finished work of Christ.

Father, you promise, for the sake of your Son, to never leave me nor forsake me. I set my hope on your steadfast love. You have started a good work in me, and you are committed to finish it when Jesus returns. *Today, I receive your peace.*

Jesus, you are the Prince of Peace. You died in my place and made peace through the blood of your cross. You made me in your likeness and know me completely. You alone can tell me who I am. *Today, I receive your peace.*

Thanks be to God!

ripture Reading

The surrender to God's good and authoritative Word.

These are the generations of Noah. Noah was a righteous man, blameless in his generation. Noah walked with God. And Noah had three sons, Shem, Ham, and Japheth.

Now the earth was corrupt in God's sight, and the earth was filled with violence. And God saw the earth, and behold, it was corrupt, for all flesh had corrupted their way on the earth. And God said to Noah, "I have determined to make an end of all flesh, for the earth is filled with violence through them. Behold, I will destroy them with the earth. Make yourself an ark of gopher wood. Make rooms in the ark, and cover it inside and out with pitch. This is how you are to make it: the length of the ark 300 cubits, its breadth 50 cubits, and its height 30 cubits. Make a roof for the ark, and finish it to a cubit above, and set the door of the ark in its side. Make it with lower, second, and third decks. For behold, I will bring a flood of waters upon the earth to destroy all flesh in which is the breath of life under heaven. Everything that is on the earth shall die. But I will establish my covenant with you, and you shall come into the ark, you, your sons, your wife, and your sor wives with you. And of every living thing of all flesh, you shall bring two of every sort into the ark to keep them alive with you. They shall be male and female. Of the birds according to their kinds, and of the animals according to their kinds, o every creeping thing of the ground, according to its kind, two of every sort shall come in to you to keep them alive. Also take with you every sort of food that is eaten, and store it up. It shall serve as food for you and for them." Noah did this; h did all that God commanded him.

Genesis 6:9-22

Prayer

An invitation to bring the needs of our bodies, hearts, and minds to the care of God.

Offer prayers for yourself and for others.

Benediction

A blessing from the authority of Scripture spoken over the people of God. The following is based on Romans 8:38-39.

For I am sure that neither death nor life, nor angels nor rulers, nor things presen nor things to come, nor powers, nor height nor depth, nor anything else in all creation, will be able to separate me from the love of God in Christ Jesus my Lor
Send me now into the world as an image bearer of God.

Daily Liturgy: Week 3, Day 3

Identity and the Self

Call to Worship

An invitation from God to all humanity to behold and join the story, work, and eternal worship of Jesus. This prayer is based on Psalm 23.

The LORD is my shepherd; I shall not want. My very life is hidden in you. Because of your abundance, I lack nothing. My soul is restless until it finds rest in you. Beside your still waters, I find rest. You, Lord, are a fountain of living water. You overflow with life, and you pour your Spirit into me. Lead me in paths of righteousness for your name's sake. May your goodness and mercy go with me today. *Amen.*

Psalm

TO THE CHOIRMASTER: ACCORDING TO MAHALATH. A MASKIL OF DAVID.

The fool says in his heart, "There is no God."
They are corrupt, doing abominable iniquity;
there is none who does good.

God looks down from heaven
on the children of man
to see if there are any who understand,
who seek after God.

They have all fallen away;
together they have become corrupt;
there is none who does good,
not even one.

Have those who work evil no knowledge,
who eat up my people as they eat bread,
and do not call upon God?

There they are, in great terror,
where there is no terror!
For God scatters the bones of him who encamps against you;
you put them to shame, for God has rejected them.

Oh, that salvation for Israel would come out of Zion!
When God restores the fortunes of his people,
let Jacob rejoice, let Israel be glad.

Psalm 53

Confession

A call to acknowledge and forsake sin against God and one another.

Father, my one hope in life and in death is that I am not my own. My body and my soul belong to you. But I have listened to the voice of the world, and let it name me. *Father, forgive me and tune my ears to hear your voice.*

You have given me dignity and worth as your image bearer. But I have listened to the lie that my value comes from status and success. Remind me that the blood of your Son speaks a better word. *Father, forgive me and tune my ears to hear your voice.*

Silently reflect on the ways you have strayed from God's gracious authority. Confess aloud and receive God's free grace through Jesus.

Assurance

An invitation to receive the assurance of a new identity in the finished work of Christ.

Jesus, you did not count equality with God a thing to be grasped, but you humbled yourself, taking the form of a servant. You lived a perfect life under the gaze of God, obeying him without wavering. You died my death, so I might live in your life. You rose again, and you are now seated at the right hand of the Father. You have surely borne my scars, and you will surely bring me home. This is my assurance and my hope. I am fully known by you alone, O Lord. *Thanks be to God!*

Scripture Reading

The surrender to God's good and authoritative Word.

Then the LORD said to Noah, "Go into the ark, you and all your household, for I have seen that you are righteous before me in this generation. Take with you seven pairs of all clean animals, the male and his mate, and a pair of the animals that are not clean, the male and his mate, and seven pairs of the birds of the heavens also, male and female, to keep their offspring alive on the face of all the earth. For in seven days I will send rain on the earth forty days and forty nights, and every living thing that I have made I will blot out from the face of the ground." And Noah did all that the LORD had commanded him.

Noah was six hundred years old when the flood of waters came upon the earth. And Noah and his sons and his wife and his sons' wives with him went into the ark to escape the waters of the flood. Of clean animals, and of animals that are not clean, and of birds, and of everything that creeps on the ground, two and two, male and female, went into the ark with Noah, as God had commanded Noah. And after seven days the waters of the flood came upon the earth.

In the six hundredth year of Noah's life, in the second month, on the seventeenth day of the month, on that day all the fountains of the great deep burst forth, and the windows of the heavens were opened. And rain fell upon the earth forty day and forty nights. On the very same day Noah and his sons, Shem and Ham and Japheth, and Noah's wife and the three wives of his sons with them entered the a they and every beast, according to its kind, and all the livestock according to thei kinds, and every creeping thing that creeps on the earth, according to its kind, and every bird, according to its kind, every winged creature. They went into the ark with Noah, two and two of all flesh in which there was the breath of life. And those that entered, male and female of all flesh, went in as God had commanded him. And the LORD shut him in.

The flood continued forty days on the earth. The waters increased and bore up the ark, and it rose high above the earth. The waters prevailed and increased greatly on the earth, and the ark floated on the face of the waters. And the water prevailed so mightily on the earth that all the high mountains under the whole heaven were covered. The waters prevailed above the mountains, covering then fifteen cubits deep. And all flesh died that moved on the earth, birds, livestock, beasts, all swarming creatures that swarm on the earth, and all mankind. Everything on the dry land in whose nostrils was the breath of life died. He blott out every living thing that was on the face of the ground, man and animals and creeping things and birds of the heavens. They were blotted out from the earth. Only Noah was left, and those who were with him in the ark. And the waters prevailed on the earth 150 days.

Genesis 7:1-24

Prayer

An invitation to bring the needs of our bodies, hearts, and minds to the care of God

Offer prayers for yourself and for others.

Benediction

A blessing from the authority of Scripture spoken over the people of God. The following is based on Philippians 4:7.

May the peace of God, which surpasses all understanding, guard my heart and mind in Christ Jesus. *Send me now into the world as an image bearer of God.*

Identity and the Self

Call to Worship

An invitation from God to all humanity to behold and join the story, work, and eternal worship of Jesus. This prayer is based on 1 Peter 2.

God, you have made us into a chosen race, a royal priesthood, a holy nation. We are a people of your possession, created to proclaim your excellencies. You have called me out of darkness and into your marvelous light. Once, we were not a people, but now we are your people. Once, I had not received mercy, but now I overflow with your mercy. *Amen.*

Psalm

TO THE CHOIRMASTER: TO DO NOT DESTROY. A MIKTAM OF DAVID, WHEN HE FLED FROM SAUL, IN THE CAVE.

Be merciful to me, O God, be merciful to me,
for in you my soul takes refuge;
in the shadow of your wings I will take refuge,
till the storms of destruction pass by.
I cry out to God Most High,
to God who fulfills his purpose for me.
He will send from heaven and save me;
he will put to shame him who tramples on me. SELAH
God will send out his steadfast love and his faithfulness!

My soul is in the midst of lions;
I lie down amid fiery beasts—
the children of man, whose teeth are spears and arrows,
whose tongues are sharp swords.

Be exalted, O God, above the heavens!
Let your glory be over all the earth!

They set a net for my steps;
my soul was bowed down.
They dug a pit in my way,
but they have fallen into it themselves. SELAH
My heart is steadfast, O God,
my heart is steadfast!
I will sing and make melody!
Awake, my glory!
Awake, O harp and lyre!
I will awake the dawn!

Daily Liturgy: Week 3, Day 4

I will give thanks to you, O Lord, among the peoples;
I will sing praises to you among the nations.
For your steadfast love is great to the heavens,
your faithfulness to the clouds.

Be exalted, O God, above the heavens!
Let your glory be over all the earth!.

Psalm 57

Confession

A call to acknowledge and forsake sin against God and one another.

Holy God, you made me out of the overflow of your love. I was made to reflect you in my relationship with others, but I have relied on my own strength and walked alone. *Forgive me, O God, for exalting myself above you.*

Holy God, you made me for your glory. I bear your image, and I only come to know myself as I find satisfaction in you. Yet I have looked to others to define me and fulfill me. *Forgive me, O God, for exalting others above you.*

Grant me the courage and humility to move toward others and make much of you.

Silently reflect on the ways you have strayed from God's gracious authority. Confess aloud and receive God's free grace through Jesus.

ssurance

An invitation to receive the assurance of a new identity in the finished work of Christ.

Father, I bring to mind your mercy, and I'm filled with hope. Through the cross and resurrection of Jesus, you brought me home from my wanderings. You've removed my mask, stripped my armor, and clothed me in the righteousness of Christ. You have called me your child, chosen and beloved. Because of you, I am made new and born again to a living hope. Jesus, you are my life, and I am most alive when I make my home in you. *Thanks be to God!*

ripture Reading

The surrender to God's good and authoritative Word.

But God remembered Noah and all the beasts and all the livestock that were with him in the ark. And God made a wind blow over the earth, and the waters subsided. The fountains of the deep and the windows of the heavens were closed, the rain from the heavens was restrained, and the waters receded from the earth continually. At the end of 150 days the waters had abated, and in the seventh month on the seventeenth day of the month, the ark came to rest on the mountains of Ararat. And the waters continued to abate until the tenth month; in the tenth month on the first day of the month, the tops of the mountains were seen.

At the end of forty days Noah opened the window of the ark that he had made and sent forth a raven. It went to and fro until the waters were dried up from the earth. Then he sent forth a dove from him, to see if the waters had subsided from the face of the ground. But the dove found no place to set her foot, and she returned to him to the ark, for the waters were still on the face of the whole earth. So he put out his hand and took her and brought her into the ark with him. He waited another seven days, and again he sent forth the dove out of the ark. And the dove came back to him in the evening, and behold, in her mouth was a freshly plucked olive leaf. So Noah knew that the waters had subsided from the earth. Then he waited another seven days and sent forth the dove, and she did not return to him anymore.

In the six hundred and first year, in the first month, the first day of the month, the waters were dried from off the earth. And Noah removed the covering of the ark and looked, and behold, the face of the ground was dry. In the second month on the twenty-seventh day of the month, the earth had dried out. Then God said to Noah, "Go out from the ark, you and your wife, and your sons and your sons' wives with you. Bring out with you every living thing that is with you of all flesh—birds and animals and every creeping thing that creeps on the earth—that they may swarm on the earth, and be fruitful and multiply on the earth." So Noah went out, and his sons and his wife and his sons' wives with him. Every beast, every creeping thing, and every bird, everything that moves on the earth, went out by families from the ark.

Genesis 8:1-19

Prayer

An invitation to bring the needs of our bodies, hearts, and minds to the care of God.

Offer prayers for yourself and for others.

Benediction

A blessing from the authority of Scripture spoken over the people of God. The following is based on Revelation 1:5-6.

To him who loves me and has freed me from my sins by his blood and made us a kingdom, priests to his God and Father, to him be glory and dominion forever and ever. *Send me now into the world as an image bearer of God.*

Daily Liturgy: Week 3, Day 5

Identity and the Self

Call to Worship

An invitation from God to all humanity to behold and join the story, work, and eterna[l] worship of Jesus. This prayer is based on Colossians 1, Psalm 36, and Psalm 139.

Jesus, you are the image of the invisible God—to see you is to see the Father. All things were created by you, through you, and for you. You made me, knit me together, and called me wonderfully made. Your thoughts toward me are precio[us] and vast. Your love toward me is rich and unending. I feast at your table and drin[k] from the river of your delights. From you comes life and light. Jesus, you are my life, and I am most alive when I make my home in you. *Amen.*

Psalm

TO THE CHOIRMASTER: ACCORDING TO JEDUTHUN. A PSALM OF DAVID.

For God alone my soul waits in silence;
from him comes my salvation.
He alone is my rock and my salvation,
my fortress; I shall not be greatly shaken.

How long will all of you attack a man
to batter him,
like a leaning wall, a tottering fence?
They only plan to thrust him down from his high position.
They take pleasure in falsehood.
They bless with their mouths,
but inwardly they curse. SELAH

For God alone, O my soul, wait in silence,
for my hope is from him.
He only is my rock and my salvation,
my fortress; I shall not be shaken.
On God rests my salvation and my glory;
my mighty rock, my refuge is God.

Trust in him at all times, O people;
pour out your heart before him;
God is a refuge for us. SELAH

Those of low estate are but a breath;
those of high estate are a delusion;
in the balances they go up;
they are together lighter than a breath.

Put no trust in extortion;
set no vain hopes on robbery;
if riches increase, set not your heart on them.

Once God has spoken;
twice have I heard this:
that power belongs to God,
and that to you, O Lord, belongs steadfast love.
For you will render to a man
according to his work.

Psalm 62

Confession

You are the one who names me. But I confess I have fractured relationship with you by running from your will. Father, your presence is my home. I belong to you and with you. I confess I am often self-centered, self-protective, and self-reliant. *Forgive me and help me return to you.*

I wear my work and reputation as righteousness. I mask myself to fit in. I am a shapeshifter. But I was never meant to bear the weight of creating my own identity. Sin has left my heart fragmented and famished. *Forgive me and help me return to you.*

Silently reflect on the ways you have strayed from God's gracious authority. Confess aloud and receive God's free grace through Jesus.

Assurance

An invitation to receive the assurance of a new identity in the finished work of Christ.

In Christ, I am a new creation. The old has passed away; the new has come. In Jesus, I am no longer the person I was, or even the person I longed to become. As a beloved and adopted child of God, he invites me to take my place at his table. I am chosen and loved. I have been rescued from every enemy of my soul. Even now, my heart condemns me, but God is greater than my heart. Nothing can separate me from his love. *Thanks be to God!*

Scripture Reading

The surrender to God's good and authoritative Word.

Then Noah built an altar to the LORD and took some of every clean animal and some of every clean bird and offered burnt offerings on the altar. And when the

LORD smelled the pleasing aroma, the LORD said in his heart, "I will never again curse the ground because of man, for the intention of man's heart is evil from his youth. Neither will I ever again strike down every living creature as I have done. While the earth remains, seedtime and harvest, cold and heat, summer and winter, day and night, shall not cease."

And God blessed Noah and his sons and said to them, "Be fruitful and multiply and fill the earth. The fear of you and the dread of you shall be upon every beast of the earth and upon every bird of the heavens, upon everything that creeps on the ground and all the fish of the sea. Into your hand they are delivered. Every moving thing that lives shall be food for you. And as I gave you the green plants, I give you everything. But you shall not eat flesh with its life, that is, its blood. And for your lifeblood I will require a reckoning: from every beast I will require it and from man. From his fellow man I will require a reckoning for the life of man.

"Whoever sheds the blood of man,
by man shall his blood be shed,
for God made man in his own image.

And you, be fruitful and multiply, increase greatly on the earth and multiply in it."

Genesis 8:20 - 9:7

Prayer

An invitation to bring the needs of our bodies, hearts, and minds to the care of God.

Offer prayers for yourself and for others.

Benediction

A blessing from the authority of Scripture spoken over the people of God.
The following is based on Romans 11:33, 36.

Oh, the depth of the riches and wisdom and knowledge of God! How unsearchab are his judgments and how inscrutable his ways! For from him and through him and to him are all things. To him be glory forever. *Send me now into the world as an image bearer of God.*

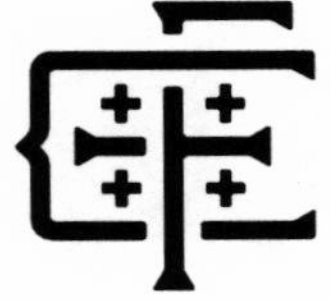

Daily Liturgies: Week 4

Identity and the Self

Daily Liturgy: Week 4, Day 1

Identity and the Self

Call to Worship

An invitation from God to all humanity to behold and join the story, work, and eternal worship of Jesus. This prayer is based on Psalms 8, 16, and 139.

O LORD, my Lord. Your name is majestic, and your glory endures forever. Who am I that you are mindful of me? God, you are my maker. You have thoughtfully and wonderfully made me. You see me and know me. All your works are perfect. Those who seek you lack no good thing. Today, I seek you, Lord. You are my chosen portion and my cup. Because you have given me yourself, I have a beautiful inheritance. *Amen.*

Psalm

TO THE CHOIRMASTER. A SONG. A PSALM.

Shout for joy to God, all the earth;
sing the glory of his name;
give to him glorious praise!
Say to God, "How awesome are your deeds!
So great is your power that your enemies come cringing to you.
All the earth worships you
and sings praises to you;
they sing praises to your name." SELAH

Come and see what God has done:
he is awesome in his deeds toward the children of man.
He turned the sea into dry land;
they passed through the river on foot.
There did we rejoice in him,
who rules by his might forever,
whose eyes keep watch on the nations—
let not the rebellious exalt themselves. SELAH

Bless our God, O peoples;
let the sound of his praise be heard,
who has kept our soul among the living
and has not let our feet slip.
For you, O God, have tested us;
you have tried us as silver is tried.
You brought us into the net;
you laid a crushing burden on our backs;
you let men ride over our heads;

we went through fire and through water;
yet you have brought us out to a place of abundance.

Psalm 66:1-12

nfession

A call to acknowledge and forsake sin against God and one another.

Father, you have made me in your image to reflect your glory. Yet I confess I regularly craft a false image and prefer to seek my own glory. *Forgive me for rejecting who I am in Christ.*

You have asked me to take up my cross, deny myself, and follow you. Yet I confess I often live for myself and follow my sinful desires. *Forgive me for rejecting who I am in Christ.*

You invite me into your peace, promising to lead me, protect me, and provide for me. Yet I confess I often plunge deeper into my anxious thoughts rather than draw near to your presence. *Forgive me for rejecting who I am in Christ.*

Silently reflect on the ways you have strayed from God's gracious authority. Confess aloud and receive God's free grace through Jesus.

surance

An invitation to receive the assurance of a new identity in the finished work of Christ.

Father, you promise, for the sake of your Son, to never leave me nor forsake me. I set my hope on your steadfast love. You have started a good work in me, and you are committed to finish it when Jesus returns. *Today, I receive your peace.*

Jesus, you are the Prince of Peace. You died in my place and made peace through the blood of your cross. You made me in your likeness and know me completely. You alone can tell me who I am. *Today, I receive your peace.*

Thanks be to God!

ripture Reading

The surrender to God's good and authoritative Word.

Then God said to Noah and to his sons with him, "Behold, I establish my covenant with you and your offspring after you, and with every living creature that is with you, the birds, the livestock, and every beast of the earth with you, as many as came out of the ark; it is for every beast of the earth. I establish my covenant with you, that never again shall all flesh be cut off by the waters of the flood, and never again shall there be a flood to destroy the earth." And God said, "This is the sign of the covenant that I make between me and you and every living creature that is with you, for all future generations: I have set my bow in the cloud, and it shall be a sign of the covenant between me and the earth. When I bring clouds over the earth anc the bow is seen in the clouds, I will remember my covenant that is between me and you and every living creature of all flesh. And the waters shall never again become a flood to destroy all flesh. When the bow is in the clouds, I will see it and remembe the everlasting covenant between God and every living creature of all flesh that is on the earth." God said to Noah, "This is the sign of the covenant that I have established between me and all flesh that is on the earth."

Genesis 9:8-17

Prayer

An invitation to bring the needs of our bodies, hearts, and minds to the care of God.

Offer prayers for yourself and for others.

Benediction

A blessing from the authority of Scripture spoken over the people of God.
The following is based on Romans 8:38-39.

For I am sure that neither death nor life, nor angels nor rulers, nor things preser nor things to come, nor powers, nor height nor depth, nor anything else in all creation, will be able to separate me from the love of God in Christ Jesus my Lor
Send me now into the world as an image bearer of God.

Daily Liturgy: Week 4, Day 2

Identity and the Self

Call to Worship

An invitation from God to all humanity to behold and join the story, work, and eternal worship of Jesus. This prayer is based on Psalm 23.

The LORD is my shepherd; I shall not want. My very life is hidden in you. Because of your abundance, I lack nothing. My soul is restless until it finds rest in you. Beside your still waters, I find rest. You, Lord, are a fountain of living water. You overflow with life, and you pour your Spirit into me. Lead me in paths of righteousness for your name's sake. May your goodness and mercy go with me today. *Amen.*

Psalm

TO THE CHOIRMASTER: WITH STRINGED INSTRUMENTS. OF DAVID.

I will come into your house with burnt offerings;
I will perform my vows to you,
that which my lips uttered
and my mouth promised when I was in trouble.
I will offer to you burnt offerings of fattened animals,
with the smoke of the sacrifice of rams;
I will make an offering of bulls and goats. SELAH

Come and hear, all you who fear God,
and I will tell what he has done for my soul.
I cried to him with my mouth,
and high praise was on my tongue.
If I had cherished iniquity in my heart,
the Lord would not have listened.
But truly God has listened;
he has attended to the voice of my prayer.

Blessed be God,
because he has not rejected my prayer
or removed his steadfast love from me!

Psalm 66:13-20

onfession

A call to acknowledge and forsake sin against God and one another.

Father, my one hope in life and in death is that I am not my own. My body and my soul belong to you. But I have listened to the voice of the world, and let it name me. *Father, forgive me and tune my ears to hear your voice.*

You have given me dignity and worth as your image bearer. But I have listened to the lie that my value comes from status and success. Remind me that the blood of your Son speaks a better word. *Father, forgive me and tune my ears to hear your voice.*

Silently reflect on the ways you have strayed from God's gracious authority. Confess aloud and receive God's free grace through Jesus.

ssurance

An invitation to receive the assurance of a new identity in the finished work of Christ.

Jesus, you did not count equality with God a thing to be grasped, but you humbled yourself, taking the form of a servant. You lived a perfect life under the gaze of God, obeying him without wavering. You died my death, so I might live in your life. You rose again, and you are now seated at the right hand of the Father. You have surely borne my scars, and you will surely bring me home. This is my assurance and my hope. I am fully known by you alone, O Lord. *Thanks be to God!*

cripture Reading

The sons of Noah who went forth from the ark were Shem, Ham, and Japheth. (Ham was the father of Canaan.) These three were the sons of Noah, and from these the people of the whole earth were dispersed.

Noah began to be a man of the soil, and he planted a vineyard. He drank of the wine and became drunk and lay uncovered in his tent. And Ham, the father of Canaan, saw the nakedness of his father and told his two brothers outside. Then Shem and Japheth took a garment, laid it on both their shoulders, and walked backward and covered the nakedness of their father. Their faces were turned backward, and they did not see their father's nakedness. When Noah awoke from his wine and knew what his youngest son had done to him, he said,

"Cursed be Canaan;
a servant of servants shall he be to his brothers."

Daily Liturgy: Week 4, Day 2

He also said,

"Blessed be the LORD, the God of Shem;
and let Canaan be his servant.
May God enlarge Japheth,
and let him dwell in the tents of Shem,
and let Canaan be his servant."

After the flood Noah lived 350 years. All the days of Noah were 950 years, and he died.

Genesis 9:18-29

Prayer

An invitation to bring the needs of our bodies, hearts, and minds to the care of God.

Offer prayers for yourself and for others.

Benediction

A blessing from the authority of Scripture spoken over the people of God.
The following is based on Philippians 4:7.

May the peace of God, which surpasses all understanding, guard my heart and my mind in Christ Jesus. *Send me now into the world as an image bearer of God.*

Identity and the Self

Call to Worship

An invitation from God to all humanity to behold and join the story, work, and eternal worship of Jesus. This prayer is based on 1 Peter 2.

God, you have made us into a chosen race, a royal priesthood, a holy nation. We ar a people of your possession, created to proclaim your excellencies. You have calle me out of darkness and into your marvelous light. Once, we were not a people, but now we are your people. Once, I had not received mercy, but now I overflow with your mercy. *Amen.*

Psalm

TO THE CHOIRMASTER: ACCORDING TO DO NOT DESTROY. A PSALM OF ASAPH. A SONG.

We give thanks to you, O God;
we give thanks, for your name is near.
We recount your wondrous deeds.

"At the set time that I appoint
I will judge with equity.
When the earth totters, and all its inhabitants,
it is I who keep steady its pillars. SELAH
I say to the boastful, 'Do not boast,'
and to the wicked, Do not lift up your horn;
do not lift up your horn on high,
or speak with haughty neck.'"

For not from the east or from the west
and not from the wilderness comes lifting up,
but it is God who executes judgment,
putting down one and lifting up another.
For in the hand of the LORD there is a cup
with foaming wine, well mixed,
and he pours out from it,
and all the wicked of the earth
shall drain it down to the dregs.

But I will declare it forever;
I will sing praises to the God of Jacob.
All the horns of the wicked I will cut off,
but the horns of the righteous shall be lifted up.

Psalm 75

Daily Liturgy: Week 4, Day 3

nfession

A call to acknowledge and forsake sin against God and one another.

Holy God, you made me out of the overflow of your love. I was made to reflect you in my relationship with others, but I have relied on my own strength and walked alone. *Forgive me, O God, for exalting myself above you.*

Holy God, you made me for your glory. I bear your image, and I only come to know myself as I find satisfaction in you. Yet I have looked to others to define me and fulfill me. *Forgive me, O God, for exalting others above you.*

Grant me the courage and humility to move toward others and make much of you.

Silently reflect on the ways you have strayed from God's gracious authority. Confess aloud and receive God's free grace through Jesus.

surance

An invitation to receive the assurance of a new identity in the finished work of Christ.

Father, I bring to mind your mercy, and I'm filled with hope. Through the cross and resurrection of Jesus, you brought me home from my wanderings. You've removed my mask, stripped my armor, and clothed me in the righteousness of Christ. You have called me your child, chosen and beloved. Because of you, I am made new and born again to a living hope. Jesus, you are my life, and I am most alive when I make my home in you. *Thanks be to God!*

ipture Reading

The surrender to God's good and authoritative Word.

These are the generations of the sons of Noah, Shem, Ham, and Japheth. Sons were born to them after the flood.

The sons of Japheth: Gomer, Magog, Madai, Javan, Tubal, Meshech, and Tiras. The sons of Gomer: Ashkenaz, Riphath, and Togarmah. The sons of Javan: Elishah, Tarshish, Kittim, and Dodanim. From these the coastland peoples spread in their lands, each with his own language, by their clans, in their nations.

The sons of Ham: Cush, Egypt, Put, and Canaan. The sons of Cush: Seba, Havilah, Sabtah, Raamah, and Sabteca. The sons of Raamah: Sheba and Dedan. Cush fathered Nimrod; he was the first on earth to be a mighty man. He was a mighty hunter before the LORD. Therefore it is said, "Like Nimrod a mighty hunter before the LORD." The beginning of his kingdom was Babel, Erech, Accad, and Calneh, in the land of Shinar. From that land he went into Assyria and built Nineveh,

Rehoboth-Ir, Calah, and Resen between Nineveh and Calah; that is the great city. Egypt fathered Ludim, Anamim, Lehabim, Naphtuhim, Pathrusim, Casluhim (from whom the Philistines came), and Caphtorim.

Canaan fathered Sidon his firstborn and Heth, and the Jebusites, the Amorites, the Girgashites, the Hivites, the Arkites, the Sinites, the Arvadites, the Zemarites, and the Hamathites. Afterward the clans of the Canaanites dispersed. And the territory of the Canaanites extended from Sidon in the direction of Gerar as far as Gaza, and in the direction of Sodom, Gomorrah, Admah, and Zeboiim, as far a Lasha. These are the sons of Ham, by their clans, their languages, their lands, an their nations.

To Shem also, the father of all the children of Eber, the elder brother of Japheth, children were born. The sons of Shem: Elam, Asshur, Arpachshad, Lud, and Ara The sons of Aram: Uz, Hul, Gether, and Mash. Arpachshad fathered Shelah; and Shelah fathered Eber. To Eber were born two sons: the name of the one was Pele for in his days the earth was divided, and his brother's name was Joktan. Joktan fathered Almodad, Sheleph, Hazarmaveth, Jerah, Hadoram, Uzal, Diklah, Obal, Abimael, Sheba, Ophir, Havilah, and Jobab; all these were the sons of Joktan. The territory in which they lived extended from Mesha in the direction of Sephar to the hill country of the east. These are the sons of Shem, by their clans, their languages, their lands, and their nations.

These are the clans of the sons of Noah, according to their genealogies, in their nations, and from these the nations spread abroad on the earth after the flood.

Genesis 10:1-32

Prayer

An invitation to bring the needs of our bodies, hearts, and minds to the care of God.

Offer prayers for yourself and for others.

Benediction

A blessing from the authority of Scripture spoken over the people of God. The following is based on Revelation 1:5-6.

To him who loves me and has freed me from my sins by his blood and made us a kingdom, priests to his God and Father, to him be glory and dominion forever ar ever. *Send me now into the world as an image bearer of God.*

Daily Liturgy: Week 4, Day 4

Identity and the Self

Call to Worship

An invitation from God to all humanity to behold and join the story, work, and eterna[l] worship of Jesus. This prayer is based on Colossians 1, Psalm 36, and Psalm 139.

Jesus, you are the image of the invisible God—to see you is to see the Father. All things were created by you, through you, and for you. You made me, knit me together, and called me wonderfully made. Your thoughts toward me are precio[us] and vast. Your love toward me is rich and unending. I feast at your table and drin[k] from the river of your delights. From you comes life and light. Jesus, you are my life, and I am most alive when I make my home in you. *Amen*

Psalm

A PSALM OF ASAPH.

O God, the nations have come into your inheritance;
they have defiled your holy temple;
they have laid Jerusalem in ruins.
They have given the bodies of your servants
to the birds of the heavens for food,
the flesh of your faithful to the beasts of the earth.
They have poured out their blood like water
all around Jerusalem,
and there was no one to bury them.
We have become a taunt to our neighbors,
mocked and derided by those around us.

How long, O LORD? Will you be angry forever?
Will your jealousy burn like fire?
Pour out your anger on the nations
that do not know you,
and on the kingdoms
that do not call upon your name!
For they have devoured Jacob
and laid waste his habitation.

Do not remember against us our former iniquities;
let your compassion come speedily to meet us,
for we are brought very low.
Help us, O God of our salvation,
for the glory of your name;
deliver us, and atone for our sins,
for your name's sake!

Why should the nations say,
"Where is their God?"
Let the avenging of the outpoured blood of your servants
be known among the nations before our eyes!

Let the groans of the prisoners come before you;
according to your great power, preserve those doomed to die!
Return sevenfold into the lap of our neighbors
the taunts with which they have taunted you, O Lord!
But we your people, the sheep of your pasture,
will give thanks to you forever;
from generation to generation we will recount your praise.

Psalm 79

nfession

A call to acknowledge and forsake sin against God and one another.

You are the one who names me. But I confess I have fractured relationship with you by running from your will. Father, your presence is my home. I belong to you and with you. I confess I am often self-centered, self-protective, and self-reliant. *Forgive me and help me return to you.*

I wear my work and reputation as righteousness. I mask myself to fit in. I am a shapeshifter. But I was never meant to bear the weight of creating my own identity. Sin has left my heart fragmented and famished. *Forgive me and help me return to you.*

Silently reflect on the ways you have strayed from God's gracious authority. Confess aloud and receive God's free grace through Jesus.

surance

An invitation to receive the assurance of a new identity in the finished work of Christ.

In Christ, I am a new creation. The old has passed away; the new has come. In Jesus, I am no longer the person I was, or even the person I longed to become. As a beloved and adopted child of God, he invites me to take my place at his table. I am chosen and loved. I have been rescued from every enemy of my soul. Even now, my heart condemns me, but God is greater than my heart. Nothing can separate me from his love. *Thanks be to God!*

Daily Liturgy: Week 4, Day 4

Scripture Reading

The surrender to God's good and authoritative Word.

Now the whole earth had one language and the same words. And as people migrated from the east, they found a plain in the land of Shinar and settled there. And they said to one another, "Come, let us make bricks, and burn them thoroughly." And they had brick for stone, and bitumen for mortar. Then they sai "Come, let us build ourselves a city and a tower with its top in the heavens, and let us make a name for ourselves, lest we be dispersed over the face of the whole earth." And the LORD came down to see the city and the tower, which the childre of man had built. And the LORD said, "Behold, they are one people, and they hav all one language, and this is only the beginning of what they will do. And nothing that they propose to do will now be impossible for them. Come, let us go down and there confuse their language, so that they may not understand one another' speech." So the LORD dispersed them from there over the face of all the earth, and they left off building the city. Therefore its name was called Babel, because there the LORD confused the language of all the earth. And from there the LORI dispersed them over the face of all the earth.

These are the generations of Shem. When Shem was 100 years old, he fathered Arpachshad two years after the flood. And Shem lived after he fathered Arpachshad 500 years and had other sons and daughters.

When Arpachshad had lived 35 years, he fathered Shelah. And Arpachshad live after he fathered Shelah 403 years and had other sons and daughters.

When Shelah had lived 30 years, he fathered Eber. And Shelah lived after he fathered Eber 403 years and had other sons and daughters.

When Eber had lived 34 years, he fathered Peleg. And Eber lived after he fathere Peleg 430 years and had other sons and daughters.

When Peleg had lived 30 years, he fathered Reu. And Peleg lived after he fathere Reu 209 years and had other sons and daughters.

When Reu had lived 32 years, he fathered Serug. And Reu lived after he fatherec Serug 207 years and had other sons and daughters.

When Serug had lived 30 years, he fathered Nahor. And Serug lived after he fathered Nahor 200 years and had other sons and daughters.

When Nahor had lived 29 years, he fathered Terah. And Nahor lived after he fathered Terah 119 years and had other sons and daughters.

When Terah had lived 70 years, he fathered Abram, Nahor, and Haran.

Genesis 11:1-26

rayer

An invitation to bring the needs of our bodies, hearts, and minds to the care of God.

Offer prayers for yourself and for others.

enediction

A blessing from the authority of Scripture spoken over the people of God.
The following is based on Romans 11:33, 36.

Oh, the depth of the riches and wisdom and knowledge of God! How unsearchable are his judgments and how inscrutable his ways! For from him and through him and to him are all things. To him be glory forever. *Send me now into the world as an image bearer of God.*

Identity and the Self

Call to Worship

An invitation from God to all humanity to behold and join the story, work, and eternal worship of Jesus. This prayer is based on Psalms 8, 16, and 139.

O LORD, my Lord. Your name is majestic, and your glory endures forever. Who am I that you are mindful of me? God, you are my maker. You have thoughtfully and wonderfully made me. You see me and know me. All your works are perfect. Those who seek you lack no good thing. Today, I seek you, Lord. You are my chosen portion and my cup. Because you have given me yourself, I have a beautiful inheritance. *Amen.*

Psalm

TO THE CHOIRMASTER: ACCORDING TO THE GITTITH. OF ASAPH.

Sing aloud to God our strength;
shout for joy to the God of Jacob!
Raise a song; sound the tambourine,
the sweet lyre with the harp.
Blow the trumpet at the new moon,
at the full moon, on our feast day.

For it is a statute for Israel,
a rule of the God of Jacob.
He made it a decree in Joseph
when he went out over the land of Egypt.
I hear a language I had not known:
"I relieved your shoulder of the burden;
your hands were freed from the basket.
In distress you called, and I delivered you;
I answered you in the secret place of thunder;
I tested you at the waters of Meribah. SELAH
Hear, O my people, while I admonish you!
O Israel, if you would but listen to me!
There shall be no strange god among you;
you shall not bow down to a foreign god.
I am the LORD your God,
who brought you up out of the land of Egypt.
Open your mouth wide, and I will fill it.

"But my people did not listen to my voice;
Israel would not submit to me.

So I gave them over to their stubborn hearts,
to follow their own counsels.
Oh, that my people would listen to me,
that Israel would walk in my ways!
I would soon subdue their enemies
and turn my hand against their foes.
Those who hate the LORD would cringe toward him,
and their fate would last forever.
But he would feed you with the finest of the wheat,
and with honey from the rock I would satisfy you."

Psalm 81

nfession

A call to acknowledge and forsake sin against God and one another.

Father, you have made me in your image to reflect your glory. Yet I confess I regularly craft a false image and prefer to seek my own glory. *Forgive me for rejecting who I am in Christ.*

You have asked me to take up my cross, deny myself, and follow you. Yet I confess I often live for myself and follow my sinful desires. *Forgive me for rejecting who I am in Christ.*

You invite me into your peace, promising to lead me, protect me, and provide for me. Yet I confess I often plunge deeper into my anxious thoughts rather than draw near to your presence. *Forgive me for rejecting who I am in Christ.*

Silently reflect on the ways you have strayed from God's gracious authority. Confess aloud and receive God's free grace through Jesus.

surance

An invitation to receive the assurance of a new identity in the finished work of Christ.

Father, you promise, for the sake of your Son, to never leave me nor forsake me. I set my hope on your steadfast love. You have started a good work in me, and you are committed to finish it when Jesus returns. *Today, I receive your peace.*

Jesus, you are the Prince of Peace. You died in my place and made peace through the blood of your cross. You made me in your likeness and know me completely. You alone can tell me who I am. *Today, I receive your peace.*

Thanks be to God!

Scripture Reading

The surrender to God's good and authoritative Word.

Now these are the generations of Terah. Terah fathered Abram, Nahor, and Hara and Haran fathered Lot. Haran died in the presence of his father Terah in the land of his kindred, in Ur of the Chaldeans. And Abram and Nahor took wives. The name of Abram's wife was Sarai, and the name of Nahor's wife, Milcah, the daughter of Haran the father of Milcah and Iscah. Now Sarai was barren; she ha no child.

Terah took Abram his son and Lot the son of Haran, his grandson, and Sarai his daughter-in-law, his son Abram's wife, and they went forth together from Ur of the Chaldeans to go into the land of Canaan, but when they came to Haran, they settled there. The days of Terah were 205 years, and Terah died in Haran.

Now the LORD said to Abram, "Go from your country and your kindred and you father's house to the land that I will show you. And I will make of you a great nati and I will bless you and make your name great, so that you will be a blessing. I wi bless those who bless you, and him who dishonors you I will curse, and in you all the families of the earth shall be blessed."

Genesis 11:27 - 12:3

Prayer

An invitation to bring the needs of our bodies, hearts, and minds to the care of God.

Offer prayers for yourself and for others.

Benediction

A blessing from the authority of Scripture spoken over the people of God.
The following is based on Romans 8:38-39.

For I am sure that neither death nor life, nor angels nor rulers, nor things preser nor things to come, nor powers, nor height nor depth, nor anything else in all creation, will be able to separate me from the love of God in Christ Jesus my Lor
Send me now into the world as an image bearer of God.

Session 3

What Does It Mean To Be Us?

Session 3

What Does It Mean To Be Us?

Call to Worship

As you begin, have someone pray this prayer out loud for the group. This praye is based on 1 Peter 2.

God, you have made us into a chosen race, a royal priesthood, a holy nation. We are a people of your possession, created to proclaim your excellencies. You hav called us out of darkness and into your marvelous light. Once, we were not a people, but now we are your people. Once, we had not received mercy, but now overflow with your mercy. *Amen.*

Bible Conversation

Have someone read the following Scripture and discussion question out loud. Spend up to 5 minutes in discussion.

Then the LORD God said, "It is not good that man should be alone; I will make him helper fit for him."... So the LORD God caused a deep sleep to fall upon the man, an while he slept took one of his ribs and closed up its place with flesh. And the rib tha the LORD God had taken from the man he made into a woman and brought her tc the man. Then the man said,

"This at last is bone of my bones and flesh of my flesh;
she shall be called Woman,
because she was taken out of Man." Genesis 2:18, 21-23

▶ ***In your own words, what does this passage teach us about our need for other Why is it not good for us to be alone?***

Training Notes

Watch the video entitled "What Does It Mean To Be Us?" found at *frontlinechurch.com/formation*. Use the notes below and fill in the blanks to follow along with the video.

> *I did examine myself. Solitude did increase my perception. But here's the tricky thing—when I applied my increased perception to myself, I lost my identity. With no audience, no one to perform for, I was just there. There was no need to define myself; I became irrelevant. The moon was the minute hand, the seasons the hour hand. I didn't even have a name.*
> **Christopher Knight as quoted by Michael Finkel, "The Strange & Curious Tale of the Last True Hermit"**

We tend to think that our identity is discovered in isolation. But in reality, the mo isolated we become, the more we lose ourselves.

You cannot be a human by yourself. Your very existence depends on a community, and always has. You cannot conceive of yourself in isolation... A community gives the language necessary for comprehending identity, and a community engages each of us in dialogue, telling us who we are and how we fit into a larger story. **Klyne Snodgrass, *Who God Says You Are***

We Are ______________________________

Then the LORD God said, "It is not good that man should be alone; I will make him a helper fit for him." **Genesis 2:18**

Humans were created to be in relationships, and we cannot understand who we are apart from others. We were given an identity from our family of origin. And even if we find ourselves rejecting that identity later in life, we are still massively influenced by it.

We are expected to develop our own opinions, outlook, stances to things, to a considerable degree through solitary reflection. But this is not how things work with important issues, such as the definition of our identity. We define this always in dialogue with, sometimes in struggle against, the identities our significant others want to recognize in us. And even when we outgrow some of the latter—our parents, for instance—and they disappear from our lives, the conversation with them continues within us as long as we live.
Charles Taylor, *The Ethics of Authenticity*

We innately imitate the behavior of those around us, sometimes without even realizing the influence of others on us.

Human children have a strong social motivation to 'be like' the other. The very act of imitating and being imitated seems to provide its own reward... Through imitation infants become like us.
Andrew Meltzoff and Peter Marshall, "Human Infant Imitation as a Social Survival Circuit"

We Don't know ourselves as well as we think

No one can look at their own face without seeing it in a reflection. No one hears their voice the same way it sounds through someone else's ears. We need others to give us a clearer picture of ourselves and our identity.

We have a profound capacity for self-deception. According to Scripture, nothing is harder to know than our own selves.

The heart is deceitful above all things, and desperately sick; who can understand? **Jeremiah 17:9**

We Long To Be Seen & Known

In order to know yourself and be yourself, you need to be known intimately and personally by others. But it doesn't end there. You also need to be truly loved by them. Being known and loved are the key ingredients to every personal identity worth inhabiting. **Brian Rosner, *How To Find Yourself***

Humans were made to know and be known. Personal identity does no good locked away in the dungeon. We find fulfillment when others come to know the "true us."

We all are born into the world looking for someone looking for us, and... we remain in this mode of searching for the rest of our lives.
Curt Thompson, *The Soul of Shame*

There is only one who will ever see us truly as we are and receive us freely. God knows us better than we will ever know ourselves. Only his love has the power transform us into his likeness.

Discussion

Have someone read aloud the following excerpt from *Speaking Truth In Love: Counsel in Community* by David Powlison. Then answer the accompanying discussion questions.

The Lord's people are called to help each other grow up. We are called to know an be known by each other. We are called to counsel each other, to be change agents each other's lives. We are called to speak the truth in love, and make a difference a brothers and sisters, shepherds and sheep...

Christian faith has intrinsic depth and an essential call to counseling wisdom, whether or not we've gotten the message yet. Our experience of church—locally, nationally, or globally—might appear worlds apart from "the church" as the Bible describes it. But what else is new? Our individual lives appear worlds apart from Jesus' life.

To pick one example, Jesus is a wonderful counselor. He cuts to the heart. He's inconceivably generous and merciful. He's eminently approachable. He asks great questions. He's fiercely tough-minded. And he turns lives upside down. In comparison, we might be bumbling, misguided, ignorant, ineffectual, harsh, or timid.

We might not even want to think of ourselves as counselors—though from Jesus' point of view, all of us are always counselors, whether foolish or wise. Sure, we've got a long way to go. But it is into that image of Jesus that we are all being transformed. It is our joy that such a transformation turns churches into communities of wise love...

One big reason we don't grasp the counseling call of the church is that we wear blinders when it comes to Word ministry. We rightly see that public ministry from the pulpit is crucial, but we often fail to see that interpersonal ministry in conversations is equally so. In fact, the quality of conversations in the church is proof of whether public ministry is succeeding or failing to achieve Christ's goals.

Answer the following questions.

How have you benefited from the wise counsel of Christians? How have you offered that same gift to others?

What scares you or encourages you about the Bible's call for Christians to help one another grow up by speaking truth in love?

ercise

If gathering as a larger group, break into smaller groups of three to four for this exercise. Set a timer for five minutes. Each person should silently fill in the squares and circles below, using the provided guidelines. After the five minutes, each person in the small group should share one square and one circle as a way to practice sharing your story with others.

Three Squares

Think about three people who have had the most significant influence on your life. Think holistically, including your learning, your spiritual growth, and the entire timeline of your life. Write down one name in each of the three squares.

Five Circles

Select five defining moments from your life. Think of a "defining" moment as a moment or event that significantly shaped who you are today. Write down one i each of the five circles.

If you broke into smaller groups, now gather back together as one large grou Answer the following question.

- ***Would anyone like to share a way you were moved or encouraged by someon else as they shared their story?***

Benediction

To conclude your time, pray this prayer out loud together, based on Revelation 1:5-6.

To him who loves us and has freed us from our sins by his blood and made us a kingdom, priests to his God and Father, to him be glory and dominion forever a ever. *Amen*

Daily Liturgies: Week 5

Identity and the World

Daily Liturgy: Week 5, Day 1

Identity and the World

Call to Worship

An invitation from God to all humanity to behold and join the story, work, and eternal worship of Jesus. This prayer is based on Psalm 23.

The LORD is my shepherd; I shall not want. My very life is hidden in you. Because of your abundance, I lack nothing. My soul is restless until it finds rest in you. Beside your still waters, I find rest. You, Lord, are a fountain of living water. You overflow with life, and you pour your Spirit into me. Lead me in paths of righteousness for your name's sake. May your goodness and mercy go with me today. *Amen.*

Psalm

A MASKIL OF ETHAN THE EZRAHITE.

I will sing of the steadfast love of the LORD, forever;
with my mouth I will make known your faithfulness to all generations.
For I said, "Steadfast love will be built up forever;
in the heavens you will establish your faithfulness."
You have said, "I have made a covenant with my chosen one;
I have sworn to David my servant:
'I will establish your offspring forever,
and build your throne for all generations.'" SELAH

Let the heavens praise your wonders, O LORD,
your faithfulness in the assembly of the holy ones!
For who in the skies can be compared to the LORD?
Who among the heavenly beings is like the LORD,
a God greatly to be feared in the council of the holy ones,
and awesome above all who are around him?
O LORD God of hosts,
who is mighty as you are, O LORD,
with your faithfulness all around you?
You rule the raging of the sea;
when its waves rise, you still them.
You crushed Rahab like a carcass;
you scattered your enemies with your mighty arm.
The heavens are yours; the earth also is yours;
the world and all that is in it, you have founded them.
The north and the south, you have created them;
Tabor and Hermon joyously praise your name.
You have a mighty arm;
strong is your hand, high your right hand.
Righteousness and justice are the foundation of your throne;

steadfast love and faithfulness go before you.
Blessed are the people who know the festal shout,
who walk, O LORD, in the light of your face,
who exult in your name all the day
and in your righteousness are exalted.
For you are the glory of their strength;
by your favor our horn is exalted.
For our shield belongs to the LORD,
our king to the Holy One of Israel.

Psalm 89:1-18

nfession

A call to acknowledge and forsake sin against God and one another.

Father, my one hope in life and in death is that I am not my own. My body and my soul belong to you. But I have listened to the voice of the world, and let it name me. *Father, forgive me and tune my ears to hear your voice.*

You have given me dignity and worth as your image bearer. But I have listened to the lie that my value comes from status and success. Remind me that the blood of your Son speaks a better word. *Father, forgive me and tune my ears to hear your voice.*

Silently reflect on the ways you have strayed from God's gracious authority. Confess aloud and receive God's free grace through Jesus.

surance

An invitation to receive the assurance of a new identity in the finished work of Christ.

Jesus, you did not count equality with God a thing to be grasped, but you humbled yourself, taking the form of a servant. You lived a perfect life under the gaze of God, obeying him without wavering. You died my death, so I might live in your life. You rose again, and you are now seated at the right hand of the Father. You have surely borne my scars, and you will surely bring me home. This is my assurance and my hope. I am fully known by you alone, O Lord. *Thanks be to God!*

ripture Reading

The surrender to God's good and authoritative Word.

That which was from the beginning, which we have heard, which we have seen with our eyes, which we looked upon and have touched with our hands, concerning the word of life—the life was made manifest, and we have seen it, and testify to it and proclaim to you the eternal life, which was with the Father and was made manifest to us—that which we have seen and heard we proclaim also to yo so that you too may have fellowship with us; and indeed our fellowship is with th Father and with his Son Jesus Christ. And we are writing these things so that ou joy may be complete.

This is the message we have heard from him and proclaim to you, that God is lig and in him is no darkness at all. If we say we have fellowship with him while we walk in darkness, we lie and do not practice the truth. But if we walk in the light, he is in the light, we have fellowship with one another, and the blood of Jesus his Son cleanses us from all sin. If we say we have no sin, we deceive ourselves, and the truth is not in us. If we confess our sins, he is faithful and just to forgive us ou sins and to cleanse us from all unrighteousness. If we say we have not sinned, w make him a liar, and his word is not in us.

1 John 1:1-10

Prayer

An invitation to bring the needs of our bodies, hearts, and minds to the care of God.

Offer prayers for yourself and for others.

Benediction

A blessing from the authority of Scripture spoken over the people of God.
The following is based on Philippians 4:7.

May the peace of God, which surpasses all understanding, guard my heart and mind in Christ Jesus. *Send me now into the world as an image bearer of God.*

Daily Liturgy: Week 5, Day 2

Identity and the World

Call to Worship

An invitation from God to all humanity to behold and join the story, work, and eternal worship of Jesus. This prayer is based on 1 Peter 2.

God, you have made us into a chosen race, a royal priesthood, a holy nation. We are a people of your possession, created to proclaim your excellencies. You have called me out of darkness and into your marvelous light. Once, we were not a people, but now we are your people. Once, I had not received mercy, but now I overflow with your mercy. *Amen.*

Psalm

Of old you spoke in a vision to your godly one, and said:
"I have granted help to one who is mighty;
I have exalted one chosen from the people.
I have found David, my servant;
with my holy oil I have anointed him,
so that my hand shall be established with him;
my arm also shall strengthen him.
The enemy shall not outwit him;
the wicked shall not humble him.
I will crush his foes before him
and strike down those who hate him.
My faithfulness and my steadfast love shall be with him,
and in my name shall his horn be exalted.
I will set his hand on the sea
and his right hand on the rivers.
He shall cry to me, 'You are my Father,
my God, and the Rock of my salvation.'
And I will make him the firstborn,
the highest of the kings of the earth.
My steadfast love I will keep for him forever,
and my covenant will stand firm for him.
I will establish his offspring forever
and his throne as the days of the heavens.
If his children forsake my law
and do not walk according to my rules,
if they violate my statutes
and do not keep my commandments,
then I will punish their transgression with the rod
and their iniquity with stripes,
but I will not remove from him my steadfast love

or be false to my faithfulness.
I will not violate my covenant
or alter the word that went forth from my lips.
Once for all I have sworn by my holiness;
I will not lie to David.
His offspring shall endure forever,
his throne as long as the sun before me.
Like the moon it shall be established forever,
a faithful witness in the skies." SELAH

Psalm 89:19-37

nfession

A call to acknowledge and forsake sin against God and one another.

Holy God, you made me out of the overflow of your love. I was made to reflect you in my relationship with others, but I have relied on my own strength and walked alone. *Forgive me, O God, for exalting myself above you.*

Holy God, you made me for your glory. I bear your image, and I only come to know myself as I find satisfaction in you. Yet I have looked to others to define me and fulfill me. *Forgive me, O God, for exalting others above you.*

Grant me the courage and humility to move toward others and make much of you.

Silently reflect on the ways you have strayed from God's gracious authority. Confess aloud and receive God's free grace through Jesus.

surance

An invitation to receive the assurance of a new identity in the finished work of Christ.

Father, I bring to mind your mercy, and I'm filled with hope. Through the cross and resurrection of Jesus, you brought me home from my wanderings. You've removed my mask, stripped my armor, and clothed me in the righteousness of Christ. You have called me your child, chosen and beloved. Because of you, I am made new and born again to a living hope. Jesus, you are my life, and I am most alive when I make my home in you. *Thanks be to God!*

ipture Reading

The surrender to God's good and authoritative Word.

My little children, I am writing these things to you so that you may not sin. But if anyone does sin, we have an advocate with the Father, Jesus Christ the righteous. He is the propitiation for our sins, and not for ours only but also for the sins of the whole world. And by this we know that we have come to know him, if we keep his commandments. Whoever says "I know him" but does not keep his commandmen is a liar, and the truth is not in him, but whoever keeps his word, in him truly the love of God is perfected. By this we may know that we are in him: whoever says he abides in him ought to walk in the same way in which he walked.

1 John 2:1-6

Prayer

An invitation to bring the needs of our bodies, hearts, and minds to the care of God

Offer prayers for yourself and for others.

Benediction

A blessing from the authority of Scripture spoken over the people of God.
The following is based on Revelation 1:5-6.

To him who loves me and has freed me from my sins by his blood and made us a kingdom, priests to his God and Father, to him be glory and dominion forever ar ever. *Send me now into the world as an image bearer of God.*

Daily Liturgy: Week 5, Day 3

Identity and the World

Call to Worship

An invitation from God to all humanity to behold and join the story, work, and etern worship of Jesus. This prayer is based on Colossians 1, Psalm 36, and Psalm 139.

Jesus, you are the image of the invisible God—to see you is to see the Father. All things were created by you, through you, and for you. You made me, knit me together, and called me wonderfully made. Your thoughts toward me are precio and vast. Your love toward me is rich and unending. I feast at your table and dri from the river of your delights. From you comes life and light. Jesus, you are my life, and I am most alive when I make my home in you. *Amen.*

Psalm

But now you have cast off and rejected;
you are full of wrath against your anointed.
You have renounced the covenant with your servant;
you have defiled his crown in the dust.
You have breached all his walls;
you have laid his strongholds in ruins.
All who pass by plunder him;
he has become the scorn of his neighbors.
You have exalted the right hand of his foes;
you have made all his enemies rejoice.
You have also turned back the edge of his sword,
and you have not made him stand in battle.
You have made his splendor to cease
and cast his throne to the ground.
You have cut short the days of his youth;
you have covered him with shame. SELAH

How long, O LORD? Will you hide yourself forever?
How long will your wrath burn like fire?
Remember how short my time is!
For what vanity you have created all the children of man!
What man can live and never see death?
Who can deliver his soul from the power of Sheol? SELAH

Lord, where is your steadfast love of old,
which by your faithfulness you swore to David?
Remember, O Lord, how your servants are mocked,
and how I bear in my heart the insults of all the many nations,
with which your enemies mock, O LORD,
with which they mock the footsteps of your anointed.

Blessed be the LORD forever!
Amen and Amen.

Psalm 89:38-52

nfession

A call to acknowledge and forsake sin against God and one another.

You are the one who names me. But I confess I have fractured relationship with you by running from your will. Father, your presence is my home. I belong to you and with you. I confess I am often self-centered, self-protective, and self-reliant. *Forgive me and help me return to you.*

I wear my work and reputation as righteousness. I mask myself to fit in. I am a shapeshifter. But I was never meant to bear the weight of creating my own identity. Sin has left my heart fragmented and famished. *Forgive me and help me return to you.*

Silently reflect on the ways you have strayed from God's gracious authority. Confess aloud and receive God's free grace through Jesus.

surance

An invitation to receive the assurance of a new identity in the finished work of Christ.

In Christ, I am a new creation. The old has passed away; the new has come. In Jesus, I am no longer the person I was, or even the person I longed to become. As a beloved and adopted child of God, he invites me to take my place at his table. I am chosen and loved. I have been rescued from every enemy of my soul. Even now, my heart condemns me, but God is greater than my heart. Nothing can separate me from his love. *Thanks be to God!*

ipture Reading

The surrender to God's good and authoritative Word.

Beloved, I am writing you no new commandment, but an old commandment that you had from the beginning. The old commandment is the word that you have heard. At the same time, it is a new commandment that I am writing to you, which is true in him and in you, because the darkness is passing away and the true light is already shining. Whoever says he is in the light and hates his brother is still in darkness. Whoever loves his brother abides in the light, and in him there is no cause for stumbling. But whoever hates his brother is in the darkness and walks in the darkness, and does not know where he is going, because the darkness has blinded his eyes.

Daily Liturgy: Week 5, Day 3

I am writing to you, little children,
because your sins are forgiven for his name's sake.
I am writing to you, fathers,
because you know him who is from the beginning.
I am writing to you, young men,
because you have overcome the evil one.
I write to you, children,
because you know the Father.
I write to you, fathers,
because you know him who is from the beginning.
I write to you, young men,
because you are strong,
and the word of God abides in you,
and you have overcome the evil one.

1 John 2:7-14

Prayer

An invitation to bring the needs of our bodies, hearts, and minds to the care of God

Offer prayers for yourself and for others.

Benediction

A blessing from the authority of Scripture spoken over the people of God. The following is based on Romans 11:33, 36.

Oh, the depth of the riches and wisdom and knowledge of God! How unsearchab are his judgments and how inscrutable his ways! For from him and through him and to him are all things. To him be glory forever. *Send me now into the world as an image bearer of God.*

Daily Liturgy: Week 5, Day 4

Identity and the World

Call to Worship

An invitation from God to all humanity to behold and join the story, work, and eternal worship of Jesus. This prayer is based on Psalms 8, 16, and 139.

O LORD, my Lord. Your name is majestic, and your glory endures forever. Who am I that you are mindful of me? God, you are my maker. You have thoughtfully and wonderfully made me. You see me and know me. All your works are perfect. Those who seek you lack no good thing. Today, I seek you, Lord. You are my chose portion and my cup. Because you have given me yourself, I have a beautiful inheritance. *Amen.*

Psalm

A PSALM. A SONG FOR THE SABBATH.

It is good to give thanks to the LORD,
to sing praises to your name, O Most High;
to declare your steadfast love in the morning,
and your faithfulness by night,
to the music of the lute and the harp,
to the melody of the lyre.
For you, O LORD, have made me glad by your work;
at the works of your hands I sing for joy.

How great are your works, O LORD!
Your thoughts are very deep!
The stupid man cannot know;
the fool cannot understand this:
that though the wicked sprout like grass
and all evildoers flourish,
they are doomed to destruction forever;
but you, O LORD, are on high forever.
For behold, your enemies, O LORD,
for behold, your enemies shall perish;
all evildoers shall be scattered.

But you have exalted my horn like that of the wild ox;
you have poured over me fresh oil.
My eyes have seen the downfall of my enemies;
my ears have heard the doom of my evil assailants.

The righteous flourish like the palm tree
and grow like a cedar in Lebanon.

They are planted in the house of the LORD;
they flourish in the courts of our God.
They still bear fruit in old age;
they are ever full of sap and green,
to declare that the LORD is upright;
he is my rock, and there is no unrighteousness in him.

Psalm 92

nfession

A call to acknowledge and forsake sin against God and one another.

Father, you have made me in your image to reflect your glory. Yet I confess I regularly craft a false image and prefer to seek my own glory. *Forgive me for rejecting who I am in Christ.*

You have asked me to take up my cross, deny myself, and follow you. Yet I confess I often live for myself and follow my sinful desires. *Forgive me for rejecting who I am in Christ.*

You invite me into your peace, promising to lead me, protect me, and provide for me. Yet I confess I often plunge deeper into my anxious thoughts rather than draw near to your presence. *Forgive me for rejecting who I am in Christ.*

Silently reflect on the ways you have strayed from God's gracious authority. Confess aloud and receive God's free grace through Jesus.

surance

An invitation to receive the assurance of a new identity in the finished work of Christ.

Father, you promise, for the sake of your Son, to never leave me nor forsake me. I set my hope on your steadfast love. You have started a good work in me, and you are committed to finish it when Jesus returns. *Today, I receive your peace.*

Jesus, you are the Prince of Peace. You died in my place and made peace through the blood of your cross. You made me in your likeness and know me completely. You alone can tell me who I am. *Today, I receive your peace.*

Thanks be to God!

Daily Liturgy: Week 5, Day 4

Scripture Reading

The surrender to God's good and authoritative Word.

Do not love the world or the things in the world. If anyone loves the world, the lo of the Father is not in him. For all that is in the world—the desires of the flesh an the desires of the eyes and pride of life—is not from the Father but is from the world. And the world is passing away along with its desires, but whoever does th will of God abides forever.

Children, it is the last hour, and as you have heard that antichrist is coming, so now many antichrists have come. Therefore we know that it is the last hour. The went out from us, but they were not of us; for if they had been of us, they would have continued with us. But they went out, that it might become plain that they all are not of us. But you have been anointed by the Holy One, and you all have knowledge. I write to you, not because you do not know the truth, but because y know it, and because no lie is of the truth. Who is the liar but he who denies that Jesus is the Christ? This is the antichrist, he who denies the Father and the Son. N one who denies the Son has the Father. Whoever confesses the Son has the Fath also. Let what you heard from the beginning abide in you. If what you heard fro the beginning abides in you, then you too will abide in the Son and in the Father. And this is the promise that he made to us—eternal life.

I write these things to you about those who are trying to deceive you. But the anointing that you received from him abides in you, and you have no need that anyone should teach you. But as his anointing teaches you about everything, an is true, and is no lie—just as it has taught you, abide in him.

1 John 2:15-27

Prayer

An invitation to bring the needs of our bodies, hearts, and minds to the care of God

Offer prayers for yourself and for others.

Benediction

A blessing from the authority of Scripture spoken over the people of God.
The following is based on Romans 8:38-39.

For I am sure that neither death nor life, nor angels nor rulers, nor things prese nor things to come, nor powers, nor height nor depth, nor anything else in all creation, will be able to separate me from the love of God in Christ Jesus my Lor *Send me now into the world as an image bearer of God.*

Daily Liturgy: Week 5, Day 5

Identity and the World

Call to Worship

An invitation from God to all humanity to behold and join the story, work, and eternal worship of Jesus. This prayer is based on Psalm 23.

The LORD is my shepherd; I shall not want. My very life is hidden in you. Becaus of your abundance, I lack nothing. My soul is restless until it finds rest in you. Beside your still waters, I find rest. You, Lord, are a fountain of living water. You overflow with life, and you pour your Spirit into me. Lead me in paths of righteousness for your name's sake. May your goodness and mercy go with me today. *Amen.*

Psalm

Oh sing to the LORD a new song;
sing to the LORD, all the earth!
Sing to the LORD, bless his name;
tell of his salvation from day to day.
Declare his glory among the nations,
his marvelous works among all the peoples!
For great is the LORD, and greatly to be praised;
he is to be feared above all gods.
For all the gods of the peoples are worthless idols,
but the LORD made the heavens.
Splendor and majesty are before him;
strength and beauty are in his sanctuary.

Ascribe to the LORD, O families of the peoples,
ascribe to the LORD glory and strength!
Ascribe to the LORD the glory due his name;
bring an offering, and come into his courts!
Worship the LORD in the splendor of holiness;
tremble before him, all the earth!

Say among the nations, "The LORD reigns!
Yes, the world is established; it shall never be moved;
he will judge the peoples with equity."

Let the heavens be glad, and let the earth rejoice;
let the sea roar, and all that fills it;
let the field exult, and everything in it!
Then shall all the trees of the forest sing for joy
before the LORD, for he comes,

for he comes to judge the earth.
He will judge the world in righteousness,
and the peoples in his faithfulness.

Psalm 96

Confession

A call to acknowledge and forsake sin against God and one another.

Father, my one hope in life and in death is that I am not my own. My body and my soul belong to you. But I have listened to the voice of the world, and let it name me. *Father, forgive me and tune my ears to hear your voice.*

You have given me dignity and worth as your image bearer. But I have listened to the lie that my value comes from status and success. Remind me that the blood of your Son speaks a better word. *Father, forgive me and tune my ears to hear your voice.*

Silently reflect on the ways you have strayed from God's gracious authority. Confess aloud and receive God's free grace through Jesus.

ssurance

An invitation to receive the assurance of a new identity in the finished work of Christ.

Jesus, you did not count equality with God a thing to be grasped, but you humbled yourself, taking the form of a servant. You lived a perfect life under the gaze of God, obeying him without wavering. You died my death, so I might live in your life. You rose again, and you are now seated at the right hand of the Father. You have surely borne my scars, and you will surely bring me home. This is my assurance and my hope. I am fully known by you alone, O Lord. *Thanks be to God!*

ripture Reading

The surrender to God's good and authoritative Word.

And now, little children, abide in him, so that when he appears we may have confidence and not shrink from him in shame at his coming. If you know that he is righteous, you may be sure that everyone who practices righteousness has been born of him.

See what kind of love the Father has given to us, that we should be called children of God; and so we are. The reason why the world does not know us is that it did not know him. Beloved, we are God's children now, and what we will be has not yet appeared; but we know that when he appears we shall be like him, because w shall see him as he is. And everyone who thus hopes in him purifies himself as h is pure.

Everyone who makes a practice of sinning also practices lawlessness; sin is lawlessness. You know that he appeared in order to take away sins, and in him there is no sin. No one who abides in him keeps on sinning; no one who keeps on sinning has either seen him or known him. Little children, let no one deceive you. Whoever practices righteousness is righteous, as he is righteous. Whoever makes a practice of sinning is of the devil, for the devil has been sinning from the beginning. The reason the Son of God appeared was to destroy the works of the devil. No one born of God makes a practice of sinning, for God's seed abides in him; and he cannot keep on sinning, because he has been born of God. By this it is evident who are the children of God, and who are the children of the devil: whoever does not practice righteousness is not of God, nor is the one who does not love his brother.

1 John 2:28-3:10

Prayer

An invitation to bring the needs of our bodies, hearts, and minds to the care of God

Offer prayers for yourself and for others.

Benediction

A blessing from the authority of Scripture spoken over the people of God. The following is based on Philippians 4:7.

May the peace of God, which surpasses all understanding, guard my heart and mind in Christ Jesus. *Send me now into the world as an image bearer of God.*

Daily Liturgies: Week 6

Identity and the World

Daily Liturgy: Week 6, Day 1

Identity and the World

Call to Worship

An invitation from God to all humanity to behold and join the story, work, and eternal worship of Jesus. This prayer is based on 1 Peter 2.

God, you have made us into a chosen race, a royal priesthood, a holy nation. We are a people of your possession, created to proclaim your excellencies. You have called me out of darkness and into your marvelous light. Once, we were not a people, but now we are your people. Once, I had not received mercy, but now I overflow with your mercy. *Amen.*

Psalm

A PRAYER OF ONE AFFLICTED, WHEN HE IS FAINT AND POURS OUT HIS COMPLAINT BEFORE THE LORD.

Hear my prayer, O LORD;
let my cry come to you!
Do not hide your face from me
in the day of my distress!
Incline your ear to me;
answer me speedily in the day when I call!

For my days pass away like smoke,
and my bones burn like a furnace.
My heart is struck down like grass and has withered;
I forget to eat my bread.
Because of my loud groaning
my bones cling to my flesh.
I am like a desert owl of the wilderness,
like an owl of the waste places;
I lie awake;
I am like a lonely sparrow on the housetop.
All the day my enemies taunt me;
those who deride me use my name for a curse.
For I eat ashes like bread
and mingle tears with my drink,
because of your indignation and anger;
for you have taken me up and thrown me down.
My days are like an evening shadow;
I wither away like grass.

But you, O LORD, are enthroned forever;
you are remembered throughout all generations.

Daily Liturgy: Week 6, Day 1

You will arise and have pity on Zion;
it is the time to favor her;
the appointed time has come.
For your servants hold her stones dear
and have pity on her dust.
Nations will fear the name of the LORD,
and all the kings of the earth will fear your glory.
For the LORD builds up Zion;
he appears in his glory;
he regards the prayer of the destitute
and does not despise their prayer.

Psalm 102:1-17

nfession

A call to acknowledge and forsake sin against God and one another.

Holy God, you made me out of the overflow of your love. I was made to reflect you in my relationship with others, but I have relied on my own strength and walked alone. *Forgive me, O God, for exalting myself above you.*

Holy God, you made me for your glory. I bear your image, and I only come to know myself as I find satisfaction in you. Yet I have looked to others to define me and fulfill me. *Forgive me, O God, for exalting others above you.*

Grant me the courage and humility to move toward others and make much of you.

Silently reflect on the ways you have strayed from God's gracious authority. Confess aloud and receive God's free grace through Jesus.

surance

An invitation to receive the assurance of a new identity in the finished work of Christ.

Father, I bring to mind your mercy, and I'm filled with hope. Through the cross and resurrection of Jesus, you brought me home from my wanderings. You've removed my mask, stripped my armor, and clothed me in the righteousness of Christ. You have called me your child, chosen and beloved. Because of you, I am made new and born again to a living hope. Jesus, you are my life, and I am most alive when I make my home in you. *Thanks be to God!*

Daily Liturgy: Week 6, Day 1

Scripture Reading

The surrender to God's good and authoritative Word.

For this is the message that you have heard from the beginning, that we should love one another. We should not be like Cain, who was of the evil one and murdered his brother. And why did he murder him? Because his own deeds we evil and his brother's righteous. Do not be surprised, brothers, that the world hates you. We know that we have passed out of death into life, because we love t brothers. Whoever does not love abides in death. Everyone who hates his brothe is a murderer, and you know that no murderer has eternal life abiding in him.

By this we know love, that he laid down his life for us, and we ought to lay down our lives for the brothers. But if anyone has the world's goods and sees his broth in need, yet closes his heart against him, how does God's love abide in him? Littl children, let us not love in word or talk but in deed and in truth.

By this we shall know that we are of the truth and reassure our heart before him; for whenever our heart condemns us, God is greater than our heart, and he knows everything. Beloved, if our heart does not condemn us, we have confiden before God; and whatever we ask we receive from him, because we keep his commandments and do what pleases him. And this is his commandment, that w believe in the name of his Son Jesus Christ and love one another, just as he has commanded us. Whoever keeps his commandments abides in God, and God in him. And by this we know that he abides in us, by the Spirit whom he has given u

1 John 3:11-24

Prayer

An invitation to bring the needs of our bodies, hearts, and minds to the care of God

Offer prayers for yourself and for others.

Benediction

A blessing from the authority of Scripture spoken over the people of God. The following is based on Revelation 1:5-6.

To him who loves me and has freed me from my sins by his blood and made us a kingdom, priests to his God and Father, to him be glory and dominion forever ar ever. *Send me now into the world as an image bearer of God.*

Daily Liturgy: Week 6, Day 2

Identity and the World

Call to Worship

An invitation from God to all humanity to behold and join the story, work, and etern worship of Jesus. This prayer is based on Colossians 1, Psalm 36, and Psalm 139.

Jesus, you are the image of the invisible God—to see you is to see the Father. All things were created by you, through you, and for you. You made me, knit me together, and called me wonderfully made. Your thoughts toward me are precio and vast. Your love toward me is rich and unending. I feast at your table and drin from the river of your delights. From you comes life and light. Jesus, you are my life, and I am most alive when I make my home in you. A*men.*

Psalm

Let this be recorded for a generation to come,
so that a people yet to be created may praise the LORD:
that he looked down from his holy height;
from heaven the LORD looked at the earth,
to hear the groans of the prisoners,
to set free those who were doomed to die,
that they may declare in Zion the name of the LORD,
and in Jerusalem his praise,
when peoples gather together,
and kingdoms, to worship the LORD.

He has broken my strength in midcourse;
he has shortened my days.
"O my God," I say, "take me not away
in the midst of my days—
you whose years endure
throughout all generations!"

Of old you laid the foundation of the earth,
and the heavens are the work of your hands.
They will perish, but you will remain;
they will all wear out like a garment.
You will change them like a robe, and they will pass away,
but you are the same, and your years have no end.
The children of your servants shall dwell secure;
their offspring shall be established before you.

Psalm 102:18-28

Daily Liturgy: Week 6, Day 2

---

nfession

A call to acknowledge and forsake sin against God and one another.

You are the one who names me. But I confess I have fractured relationship with you by running from your will. Father, your presence is my home. I belong to you and with you. I confess I am often self-centered, self-protective, and self-reliant. *Forgive me and help me return to you.*

I wear my work and reputation as righteousness. I mask myself to fit in. I am a shapeshifter. But I was never meant to bear the weight of creating my own identity. Sin has left my heart fragmented and famished. *Forgive me and help me return to you.*

Silently reflect on the ways you have strayed from God's gracious authority. Confess aloud and receive God's free grace through Jesus.

surance

An invitation to receive the assurance of a new identity in the finished work of Christ.

In Christ, I am a new creation. The old has passed away; the new has come. In Jesus, I am no longer the person I was, or even the person I longed to become. As a beloved and adopted child of God, he invites me to take my place at his table. I am chosen and loved. I have been rescued from every enemy of my soul. Even now, my heart condemns me, but God is greater than my heart. Nothing can separate me from his love. *Thanks be to God!*

ipture Reading

The surrender to God's good and authoritative Word.

Beloved, do not believe every spirit, but test the spirits to see whether they are from God, for many false prophets have gone out into the world. By this you know the Spirit of God: every spirit that confesses that Jesus Christ has come in the flesh is from God, and every spirit that does not confess Jesus is not from God. This is the spirit of the antichrist, which you heard was coming and now is in the world already. Little children, you are from God and have overcome them, for he who is in you is greater than he who is in the world. They are from the world; therefore they speak from the world, and the world listens to them. We are from God. Whoever knows God listens to us; whoever is not from God does not listen to us. By this we know the Spirit of truth and the spirit of error.

1 John 4:1-6

Daily Liturgy: Week 6, Day 2

Prayer

An invitation to bring the needs of our bodies, hearts, and minds to the care of God

Offer prayers for yourself and for others.

Benediction

A blessing from the authority of Scripture spoken over the people of God. The following is based on Romans 11:33, 36.

Oh, the depth of the riches and wisdom and knowledge of God! How unsearchable are his judgments and how inscrutable his ways! For from him and through him and to him are all things. To him be glory forever. *Send me now into the world as an image bearer of God.*

Daily Liturgy: Week 6, Day 3

Identity and the World

Call to Worship

An invitation from God to all humanity to behold and join the story, work, and eternal worship of Jesus. This prayer is based on Psalms 8, 16, and 139.

O LORD, my Lord. Your name is majestic, and your glory endures forever. Who am I that you are mindful of me? God, you are my maker. You have thoughtfully and wonderfully made me. You see me and know me. All your works are perfect. Those who seek you lack no good thing. Today, I seek you, Lord. You are my chose portion and my cup. Because you have given me yourself, I have a beautiful inheritance. A*men.*

Psalm

Oh give thanks to the LORD, for he is good,
for his steadfast love endures forever!
Let the redeemed of the LORD say so,
whom he has redeemed from trouble
and gathered in from the lands,
from the east and from the west,
from the north and from the south.

Some wandered in desert wastes,
finding no way to a city to dwell in;
hungry and thirsty,
their soul fainted within them.
Then they cried to the LORD in their trouble,
and he delivered them from their distress.
He led them by a straight way
till they reached a city to dwell in.
Let them thank the LORD for his steadfast love,
for his wondrous works to the children of man!
For he satisfies the longing soul,
and the hungry soul he fills with good things.

Some sat in darkness and in the shadow of death,
prisoners in affliction and in irons,
for they had rebelled against the words of God,
and spurned the counsel of the Most High.
So he bowed their hearts down with hard labor;
they fell down, with none to help.
Then they cried to the LORD in their trouble,
and he delivered them from their distress.

Daily Liturgy: Week 6, Day 3

He brought them out of darkness and the shadow of death,
and burst their bonds apart.
Let them thank the LORD for his steadfast love,
for his wondrous works to the children of man!
For he shatters the doors of bronze
and cuts in two the bars of iron.

Psalm 107:1-16

nfession

A call to acknowledge and forsake sin against God and one another.

Father, you have made me in your image to reflect your glory. Yet I confess I regularly craft a false image and prefer to seek my own glory. *Forgive me for rejecting who I am in Christ.*

You have asked me to take up my cross, deny myself, and follow you. Yet I confess I often live for myself and follow my sinful desires. *Forgive me for rejecting who I am in Christ.*

You invite me into your peace, promising to lead me, protect me, and provide for me. Yet I confess I often plunge deeper into my anxious thoughts rather than draw near to your presence. *Forgive me for rejecting who I am in Christ.*

Silently reflect on the ways you have strayed from God's gracious authority. Confess aloud and receive God's free grace through Jesus.

surance

An invitation to receive the assurance of a new identity in the finished work of Christ.

Father, you promise, for the sake of your Son, to never leave me nor forsake me. I set my hope on your steadfast love. You have started a good work in me, and you are committed to finish it when Jesus returns. *Today, I receive your peace.*

Jesus, you are the Prince of Peace. You died in my place and made peace through the blood of your cross. You made me in your likeness and know me completely. You alone can tell me who I am. *Today, I receive your peace.*

Thanks be to God!

Daily Liturgy: Week 6, Day 3

Scripture Reading

The surrender to God's good and authoritative Word.

Beloved, let us love one another, for love is from God, and whoever loves has been born of God and knows God. Anyone who does not love does not know Go because God is love. In this the love of God was made manifest among us, that God sent his only Son into the world, so that we might live through him. In this is love, not that we have loved God but that he loved us and sent his Son to be the propitiation for our sins. Beloved, if God so loved us, we also ought to love one another. No one has ever seen God; if we love one another, God abides in us and his love is perfected in us.

By this we know that we abide in him and he in us, because he has given us of his Spirit. And we have seen and testify that the Father has sent his Son to be the Savior of the world. Whoever confesses that Jesus is the Son of God, God abides him, and he in God. So we have come to know and to believe the love that God ha for us. God is love, and whoever abides in love abides in God, and God abides in him. By this is love perfected with us, so that we may have confidence for the da of judgment, because as he is so also are we in this world. There is no fear in lov but perfect love casts out fear. For fear has to do with punishment, and whoever fears has not been perfected in love. We love because he first loved us. If anyone says, "I love God," and hates his brother, he is a liar; for he who does not love his brother whom he has seen cannot love God whom he has not seen. And this commandment we have from him: whoever loves God must also love his brothe

1 John 4:7-21

Prayer

An invitation to bring the needs of our bodies, hearts, and minds to the care of God

Offer prayers for yourself and for others.

Benediction

A blessing from the authority of Scripture spoken over the people of God.
The following is based on Romans 8:38-39.

For I am sure that neither death nor life, nor angels nor rulers, nor things prese nor things to come, nor powers, nor height nor depth, nor anything else in all creation, will be able to separate me from the love of God in Christ Jesus my Lor
Send me now into the world as an image bearer of God.

Daily Liturgy: Week 6, Day 4

Identity and the World

Call to Worship

An invitation from God to all humanity to behold and join the story, work, and eternal worship of Jesus. This prayer is based on Psalm 23.

The LORD is my shepherd; I shall not want. My very life is hidden in you. Becaus of your abundance, I lack nothing. My soul is restless until it finds rest in you. Beside your still waters, I find rest. You, Lord, are a fountain of living water. You overflow with life, and you pour your Spirit into me. Lead me in paths of righteousness for your name's sake. May your goodness and mercy go with me today. *Amen.*

Psalm

Some were fools through their sinful ways,
and because of their iniquities suffered affliction;
they loathed any kind of food,
and they drew near to the gates of death.
Then they cried to the LORD in their trouble,
and he delivered them from their distress.
He sent out his word and healed them,
and delivered them from their destruction.
Let them thank the LORD for his steadfast love,
for his wondrous works to the children of man!
And let them offer sacrifices of thanksgiving,
and tell of his deeds in songs of joy!

Some went down to the sea in ships,
doing business on the great waters;
they saw the deeds of the LORD,
his wondrous works in the deep.
For he commanded and raised the stormy wind,
which lifted up the waves of the sea.
They mounted up to heaven; they went down to the depths;
their courage melted away in their evil plight;
they reeled and staggered like drunken men
and were at their wits' end.
Then they cried to the LORD in their trouble,
and he delivered them from their distress.
He made the storm be still,
and the waves of the sea were hushed.
Then they were glad that the waters were quiet,
and he brought them to their desired haven.
Let them thank the LORD for his steadfast love,

for his wondrous works to the children of man!
Let them extol him in the congregation of the people,
and praise him in the assembly of the elders.

Psalm 107:17-32

Confession

A call to acknowledge and forsake sin against God and one another.

Father, my one hope in life and in death is that I am not my own. My body and my soul belong to you. But I have listened to the voice of the world, and let it name me. *Father, forgive me and tune my ears to hear your voice.*

You have given me dignity and worth as your image bearer. But I have listened to the lie that my value comes from status and success. Remind me that the blood of your Son speaks a better word. *Father, forgive me and tune my ears to hear your voice.*

Silently reflect on the ways you have strayed from God's gracious authority. Confess aloud and receive God's free grace through Jesus.

Assurance

An invitation to receive the assurance of a new identity in the finished work of Christ.

Jesus, you did not count equality with God a thing to be grasped, but you humbled yourself, taking the form of a servant. You lived a perfect life under the gaze of God, obeying him without wavering. You died my death, so I might live in your life. You rose again, and you are now seated at the right hand of the Father. You have surely borne my scars, and you will surely bring me home. This is my assurance and my hope. I am fully known by you alone, O Lord. *Thanks be to God!*

Scripture Reading

The surrender to God's good and authoritative Word.

Everyone who believes that Jesus is the Christ has been born of God, and everyone who loves the Father loves whoever has been born of him. By this we know that we love the children of God, when we love God and obey his commandments. For this is the love of God, that we keep his commandments. And his commandments are not burdensome. For everyone who has been born of God overcomes the world. And this is the victory that has overcome the world—our faith. Who is it that overcomes the world except the one who believes that Jesus is the Son of God?

This is he who came by water and blood—Jesus Christ; not by the water only but by the water and the blood. And the Spirit is the one who testifies, because the Spirit is the truth. For there are three that testify: the Spirit and the water and the blood; and these three agree. If we receive the testimony of men, the testimony of God is greater, for this is the testimony of God that he has borne concerning his Son. Whoever believes in the Son of God has the testimony in himself. Whoever does not believe God has made him a liar, because he has not believed in the testimony that God has borne concerning his Son. And this is the testimony, that God gave us eternal life, and this life is in his Son. Whoever has the Son has life; whoever does not have the Son of God does not have life.

1 John 5:1-12

Prayer

An invitation to bring the needs of our bodies, hearts, and minds to the care of God.

Offer prayers for yourself and for others.

Benediction

A blessing from the authority of Scripture spoken over the people of God. The following is based on Philippians 4:7.

May the peace of God, which surpasses all understanding, guard my heart and m mind in Christ Jesus. *Send me now into the world as an image bearer of God.*

Daily Liturgy: Week 6, Day 5

Identity and the World

Call to Worship

An invitation from God to all humanity to behold and join the story, work, and eternal worship of Jesus. This prayer is based on 1 Peter 2.

God, you have made us into a chosen race, a royal priesthood, a holy nation. We are a people of your possession, created to proclaim your excellencies. You have called me out of darkness and into your marvelous light. Once, we were not a people, but now we are your people. Once, I had not received mercy, but now I overflow with your mercy. *Amen.*

Psalm

He turns rivers into a desert,
springs of water into thirsty ground,
a fruitful land into a salty waste,
because of the evil of its inhabitants.
He turns a desert into pools of water,
a parched land into springs of water.
And there he lets the hungry dwell,
and they establish a city to live in;
they sow fields and plant vineyards
and get a fruitful yield.
By his blessing they multiply greatly,
and he does not let their livestock diminish.

When they are diminished and brought low
through oppression, evil, and sorrow,
he pours contempt on princes
and makes them wander in trackless wastes;
but he raises up the needy out of affliction
and makes their families like flocks.
The upright see it and are glad,
and all wickedness shuts its mouth.

Whoever is wise, let him attend to these things;
let them consider the steadfast love of the LORD.

Psalm 107:33-43

Daily Liturgy: Week 6, Day 5

nfession

A call to acknowledge and forsake sin against God and one another.

Holy God, you made me out of the overflow of your love. I was made to reflect you in my relationship with others, but I have relied on my own strength and walked alone. *Forgive me, O God, for exalting myself above you.*

Holy God, you made me for your glory. I bear your image, and I only come to know myself as I find satisfaction in you. Yet I have looked to others to define me and fulfill me. *Forgive me, O God, for exalting others above you.*

Grant me the courage and humility to move toward others and make much of you.

Silently reflect on the ways you have strayed from God's gracious authority. Confess aloud and receive God's free grace through Jesus.

surance

An invitation to receive the assurance of a new identity in the finished work of Christ.

Father, I bring to mind your mercy, and I'm filled with hope. Through the cross and resurrection of Jesus, you brought me home from my wanderings. You've removed my mask, stripped my armor, and clothed me in the righteousness of Christ. You have called me your child, chosen and beloved. Because of you, I am made new and born again to a living hope. Jesus, you are my life, and I am most alive when I make my home in you. *Thanks be to God!*

ipture Reading

The surrender to God's good and authoritative Word.

I write these things to you who believe in the name of the Son of God, that you may know that you have eternal life. And this is the confidence that we have toward him, that if we ask anything according to his will he hears us. And if we know that he hears us in whatever we ask, we know that we have the requests that we have asked of him.

If anyone sees his brother committing a sin not leading to death, he shall ask, and God will give him life—to those who commit sins that do not lead to death. There is sin that leads to death; I do not say that one should pray for that. All wrongdoing is sin, but there is sin that does not lead to death.

Daily Liturgy: Week 6, Day 5

We know that everyone who has been born of God does not keep on sinning, but he who was born of God protects him, and the evil one does not touch him. We know that we are from God, and the whole world lies in the power of the evil one.

And we know that the Son of God has come and has given us understanding, so that we may know him who is true; and we are in him who is true, in his Son Jesus Christ. He is the true God and eternal life. Little children, keep yourselves from idols.

1 John 5:13-21

Prayer

An invitation to bring the needs of our bodies, hearts, and minds to the care of God

Offer prayers for yourself and for others.

Benediction

A blessing from the authority of Scripture spoken over the people of God. The following is based on Revelation 1:5-6.

To him who loves me and has freed me from my sins by his blood and made us a kingdom, priests to his God and Father, to him be glory and dominion forever and ever. *Send me now into the world as an image bearer of God.*

Session 4

What Does It Mean To Be In Christ?

Session 4

What Does It Mean To Be In Christ?

Call to Worship

As you begin, have someone pray this prayer out loud for the group.

Jesus, you are the image of the invisible God—to see you is to see the Father. All things were created by you, through you, and for you. You made us, knit us togeth and called us wonderfully made. Your thoughts toward us are precious and vast. Your love toward us is rich and unending. We feast at your table and drink from th river of your delights. From you comes life and light. Jesus, you are our life, and w are most alive when we make our home in you. *Amen.*

Bible Conversation

Have someone read the following Scripture and discussion question out loud. Spend up to 5 minutes in discussion.

> *If then you have been raised with Christ, seek the things that are above, where Christ is, seated at the right hand of God. Set your minds on things that are above, not on things that are on earth. For you have died, and your life is hidden with Christ in God. When Christ who is your life appears, then you also will appear with him in glory.* Colossians 3:1-4

▶ ***What do you think it means for our life to be hidden with Christ? If our lif is hidden in Christ, what does it look like to set our minds "on things that are above"?***

Training Notes

Watch the video entitled "What Does It Mean To Be In Christ?" found at *frontlinechurch.com/formation.* Use the notes below and fill in the blanks to follow along with the video.

> *Whoever finds his life will lose it, and whoever loses his life for my sake will find it.* Matthew 10:39

When we feel certain we have found ourselves, when we think we have discover the "true me" inside us, we are actually further away from who we really are an who we were made to be.

> *The more we get what we now call "ourselves" out of the way and let Him take us over, the more truly ourselves we become... Our real selves are all waiting for us in Him... The more I resist Him and try to live on my own, the more I become dominated by my own heredity and upbringing and surrounding and natural desires... Look for yourself, and you will find in the long run only hatred, loneliness, despair, rage, ruin, and decay. But look for*

Christ and you will find Him, and with Him everything else thrown in.
C. S. Lewis, *Mere Christianity*

Looking within to craft our own identity will only lead us further away from who we truly are. Rather, we find our life when we lose it for the sake of Jesus.

If then you have been raised with Christ, seek the things that are above, where Christ is, seated at the right hand of God. Set your minds on things that are above, not on things that are on earth. For you have died, and your life is hidden with Christ in God. When Christ who is your life appears, then you also will appear with him in glory. **Colossians 3:1-4**

Jesus transformed the idea of identity, radically centering all of life around him. Our salvation, our practices, and even our identity, only make sense in who Jesus is.

If you are in Christ, this is now the defining truth of who you are. Your life, your story, becomes enfolded by another story—Another's story. That's one way to define faith: faith means finding your identity in Christ... Being in Christ is to discover our true, God-given identity. You are alive in him, moving with him through this world, clothed in all his benefits and blessings. You are in Christ. **Rankin Wilbourne, *Union With Christ***

In Christ, We Receive a ____________________________________

When we place our faith in Jesus, God enters our story and retells it in light of his bigger and better story.

Or do you not know that the unrighteous will not inherit the kingdom of God?... And such were some of you. But you were washed, you were sanctified, you were justified in the name of the Lord Jesus Christ and by the Spirit of our God. **1 Corinthians 6:9, 11**

When we are baptized, we proclaim that we have entered a new story and taken on a new identity. His story becomes our story. Our life can't make sense apart from him.

In Christ, We Join a ______________________________________

By finding our identity in Christ, we become a part of his body, the Church. We are brought into a new family, one united by faith in Jesus.

In Christ Jesus you are all sons of God, through faith. For as many of you as were baptized into Christ have put on Christ. There is neither Jew nor Greek, there is neither slave nor free, there is no male and female, for you are all one in Christ Jesus. **Galatians 3:26-27**

This new corporate identity shapes how we relate to others. Instead of being driven by anxiety, anger, or strife, we become people shaped by the peace of Jesus

In Christ, We Become a ____________________________________

For followers of Jesus, who we were is not who we are. Even better, who we are is not who we will be.

> *Therefore, if anyone is in Christ, he is a new creation. The old has passed away; behold, the new has come.* **2 Corinthians 5:17**

We are increasingly renewed into the image of God as we put away those practices that defined how we used to live.

> *Do not lie to one another, seeing that you have put off the old self with its practices and have put on the new self, which is being renewed in knowledge after the image of its creator.* **Colossians 3:9-10**

Jesus transforms us and remakes us into his own image. He empowers us to fulfill our original design as humans, to display the glory of God, and to bring God's presence and rule to the world.

> *And we all, with unveiled face, beholding the glory of the Lord, are being transformed into the same image from one degree of glory to another. For this comes from the Lord who is the Spirit.* **2 Corinthians 3:18**

Discussion

Our culture holds to what you might call a "Choose Your Own Identity" mindset to life. But this approach falls short of its promises and fails to satisfy. Rankin Wilbourne, in his book *Union With Christ: The Way to Know and Enjoy God*, names five problems with this mindset.

Take turns reading the five problems aloud together, adapted from Wilbourne's book. Then answer the accompanying discussion question.

PROBLEM	DESCRIPTION
Paralysis	A "Choose Your Own Identity" mindset puts the accent on unlimited freedom, which often leads to paralysis. Take your career. No one wants to go back to the days of "My daddy was a farmer, so I must be a farmer." But when you can do anything, and it's up to you to choose, then that long list of possibilities, coupled with the significance of your choice, can be paralyzing. The weight of the possible is heavy indee

PROBLEM	DESCRIPTION
Anxiety	The rate of anxiety and depression is higher today than it has ever been because of increased feelings of inadequacy—rising from a social context in which success is credited to, and expected of, the autonomous individual. Or, suppose you are one of the rare individuals who actually does know what you want to do with your life. Great! Now all you have to do is go do it. And do it well. And keep it up. That's an unrelenting pressure that no amount of success can relieve because the question is always, "Now, what will you do next?" And if you don't make it or can't make it, then what? If it's all up to you, and you fail, then who do you have left to blame?
Discontentment	The idea that more choice equals more happiness is completely wrong. Increased choices have led to increased expectations of how good a good choice should be (with so many choices, surely one of them is almost perfect), which leads to increased dissatisfaction with whatever choice you end up making. Expectations have gone through the roof, and with them our rising discontentment. Take dating and marriage. With such high expectations going in, it's hard not to slip into thinking, "if only" you'd made a different choice, then you'd be happier. And you might be. But when you pit the imagined possibilities of what you don't have against the real limitations of what you do, it inevitably leads to dissatisfaction with whomever you choose. Or, it might make you reluctant to choose at all—commitment phobic. So even though we have it better than we ever have, we're less content than we've ever been.
Loss of Freedom	We long to be free. Never has a culture talked about freedom more but experienced it less. But autonomy can't set us free. It only ends up imprisoning us in the labyrinth of our constantly shifting desires. How free is a fish in a fishbowl? Yes, of course the fish is confined, but to shatter the fishbowl, to remove all constraints, would not improve the fish's situation. In fact, it would destroy him. The real question, therefore, is which boundaries will set us free?
Distant God	We can treat God as a convenient, yet distant, deity. We may co-opt God into our plans, but we don't want him making plans for us. In our quest to discover our true selves, it's hard not to see God simply as an authority figure who will constrain us and impede our freedom. In our disenchanted, pragmatically driven world, we may try to keep God on call for when we're in trouble or need help. God becomes a stagehand to the play we are writing and starring in.

Which one of these five problems describes your life experience the most, and why?

Exercise

Union with Christ provides the antidote to these problems. Identify the proble that most resonated with your life experience above. Set a five minute timer. Each person should silently read through the antidote of the particular probl listed below, adapted from Wilbourne's book. Then, in your own words, write prayer based on what you read. In your prayer, you could ask for more faith t believe your union in Christ, or give thanks for how he's already begun to wo in you. Don't worry about making it long; it can be just a few sentences. Afte the five minutes, whoever is willing can share what they wrote.

	DESCRIPTION	PRAYER
PARALYSIS VS. REST IN CHRIST	Union with Christ gives us permission to rest. We don't have to be burdened by the weight of the possible. We do have so many choices. But union with Christ says there is one choice more important than any other choice you will make: Thy will be done or my will be done? As long as your will is set on following Christ, you can rest in the choices you make. You don't have to be frozen in fear because your life is no longer in your own hands.	
ANXIETY VS. APPROVAL IN CHRIST	Union with Christ tells us you have died to that old way of trying to justify your existence by your own work. You have died to the angst that comes from thinking you're not allowed to fail, or to the feelings of inadequacy that come from believing you have. To those human questions—Am I significant? Have I done enough? Am I accepted?—the answer is "Your life is now hidden with Christ in God" (Col. 3:3). This is the precious biblical truth of justification (Gal. 2:16). You no longer have to justify your life... This doesn't mean you stop working, but it does mean you now work in a totally new way. You no longer work *for* approval; you work *from* approval.	
DISCONTENTMENT VS. CONTENTMENT IN CHRIST	To our discontentment and dissatisfaction, one united to Christ can say, "I have learned in whatever situation I am to be content. In any and every circumstance, I have learned the secret of facing plenty and hunger, abundance and need" (Phil. 4:11–12). What is this secret Paul learned? The secret is that his life is now empowered by the presence of Christ, which is why he immediately follows these words with "I can do all things through [Christ] who strengthens me" (v. 13). Union with Christ is the antidote to our discontentment.	Jesus, help m learn this contentment in you + n fear what y call me to.

	DESCRIPTION	PRAYER
LOSS OF FREEDOM VS. FREEDOM IN CHRIST	Union with Christ tells you that Jesus is the center and circumference of authentic human existence. Jesus is the center—we can't understand ourselves without understanding who he is and what he has done for us. And Jesus is the circumference—he sets the boundaries of what it means to be human. Your real identity, your real self, is waiting to be found in him. Union with Christ says you were made to be a part of God's family and that only by finding your place here will you be free. When you become a Christian, God sends the Spirit of his Son into your heart who cries out, "Abba! Father!" (Gal. 4:6). This is the great biblical truth of adoption, that in Christ, you have been adopted into God's family. Living in any family constrains your freedom, but living in this family is what you were made for. This Spirit of adoption, the Bible says, sets you free (Rom. 8:15) because you've finally found the boundaries that fit you. You have found your place. You are home.	
DISTANT GOD VS. GOD COMES CLOSE IN CHRIST	Union with Christ says God is closer and more intimate than we ever imagined. He's not a stagehand in the play you are writing and starring in. You are no longer the star of the show. It's not about you. He displaces you from the center of your life. But this new role means you get to be part of something bigger than your own autobiography. You are invited into God's story, the biggest and best story of them all. If you are in Christ, your life and your story become enfolded by another story—Another's story. You don't have to discover or craft, create or achieve, invent or reinvent your own identity. Your identity is found not deep within yourself but outside of yourself. Your self-understanding becomes inseparable from who God says you are in Christ. Who are you? Your identity is no longer a construct of your own preferences and choices, accomplishments or affiliations. You no longer stand alone. You no longer get the credit or the blame, the applause or the jeers.	

End your time by praying for one another, that you would more fully be shaped by your identity in Christ. You do NOT need to use your prayers you wrote for the exercise.

Benediction

To conclude your time, pray this prayer out loud together. The following is base on Romans 11:33-36.

Oh, the depth of the riches and wisdom and knowledge of God! How unsearchal are his judgments and how inscrutable his ways! For from him and through him and to him are all things. To him be glory forever. *Amen.*

Daily Liturgies: Week 7

Identity and the Gospel

Daily Liturgy: Week 7, Day 1

Identity and the Gospel

Call to Worship

An invitation from God to all humanity to behold and join the story, work, and etern worship of Jesus. This prayer is based on Colossians 1, Psalm 36, and Psalm 139.

Jesus, you are the image of the invisible God—to see you is to see the Father. All things were created by you, through you, and for you. You made me, knit me together, and called me wonderfully made. Your thoughts toward me are preci and vast. Your love toward me is rich and unending. I feast at your table and dri from the river of your delights. From you comes life and light. Jesus, you are my life, and I am most alive when I make my home in you. *Amen.*

Psalm

Praise the LORD!
Blessed is the man who fears the LORD,
who greatly delights in his commandments!
His offspring will be mighty in the land;
the generation of the upright will be blessed.
Wealth and riches are in his house,
and his righteousness endures forever.
Light dawns in the darkness for the upright;
he is gracious, merciful, and righteous.
It is well with the man who deals generously and lends;
who conducts his affairs with justice.
For the righteous will never be moved;
he will be remembered forever.
He is not afraid of bad news;
his heart is firm, trusting in the LORD.
His heart is steady; he will not be afraid,
until he looks in triumph on his adversaries.
He has distributed freely; he has given to the poor;
his righteousness endures forever;
his horn is exalted in honor.
The wicked man sees it and is angry;
he gnashes his teeth and melts away;
the desire of the wicked will perish!

Psalm 112

nfession

A call to acknowledge and forsake sin against God and one another.

You are the one who names me. But I confess I have fractured relationship with you by running from your will. Father, your presence is my home. I belong to you and with you. I confess I am often self-centered, self-protective, and self-reliant. *Forgive me and help me return to you.*

I wear my work and reputation as righteousness. I mask myself to fit in. I am a shapeshifter. But I was never meant to bear the weight of creating my own identity. Sin has left my heart fragmented and famished. *Forgive me and help me return to you.*

Silently reflect on the ways you have strayed from God's gracious authority. Confess aloud and receive God's free grace through Jesus.

urance

An invitation to receive the assurance of a new identity in the finished work of Christ.

In Christ, I am a new creation. The old has passed away; the new has come. In Jesus, I am no longer the person I was, or even the person I longed to become. As a beloved and adopted child of God, he invites me to take my place at his table. I am chosen and loved. I have been rescued from every enemy of my soul. Even now, my heart condemns me, but God is greater than my heart. Nothing can separate me from his love. *Thanks be to God!*

ipture Reading

The surrender to God's good and authoritative Word.

Then Jesus told his disciples, "If anyone would come after me, let him deny himself and take up his cross and follow me. For whoever would save his life will lose it, but whoever loses his life for my sake will find it. For what will it profit a man if he gains the whole world and forfeits his soul? Or what shall a man give in return for his soul? For the Son of Man is going to come with his angels in the glory of his Father, and then he will repay each person according to what he has done. Truly, I say to you, there are some standing here who will not taste death until they see the Son of Man coming in his kingdom."

Matthew 16:24-28

Daily Liturgy: Week 7, Day 1

Prayer

An invitation to bring the needs of our bodies, hearts, and minds to the care of Go

Offer prayers for yourself and for others.

Benediction

A blessing from the authority of Scripture spoken over the people of God. The following is based on Romans 11:33, 36.

Oh, the depth of the riches and wisdom and knowledge of God! How unsearcha are his judgments and how inscrutable his ways! For from him and through hin and to him are all things. To him be glory forever. *Send me now into the world as an image bearer of God.*

Daily Liturgy: Week 7, Day 2

Identity and the Gospel

Call to Worship

An invitation from God to all humanity to behold and join the story, work, and eternal worship of Jesus. This prayer is based on Psalms 8, 16, and 139.

O LORD, my Lord. Your name is majestic, and your glory endures forever. Who am I that you are mindful of me? God, you are my maker. You have thoughtfully and wonderfully made me. You see me and know me. All your works are perfect. Those who seek you lack no good thing. Today, I seek you, Lord. You are my chose portion and my cup. Because you have given me yourself, I have a beautiful inheritance. *Amen.*

Psalm

A SONG OF ASCENTS.

In my distress I called to the LORD,
and he answered me.
Deliver me, O LORD,
from lying lips,
from a deceitful tongue.

What shall be given to you,
and what more shall be done to you,
you deceitful tongue?
A warrior's sharp arrows,
with glowing coals of the broom tree!

Woe to me, that I sojourn in Meshech,
that I dwell among the tents of Kedar!
Too long have I had my dwelling
among those who hate peace.
I am for peace,
but when I speak, they are for war!

Psalm 120

Confession

A call to acknowledge and forsake sin against God and one another.

Father, you have made me in your image to reflect your glory. Yet I confess I regularly craft a false image and prefer to seek my own glory. *Forgive me for rejecting who I am in Christ.*

You have asked me to take up my cross, deny myself, and follow you. Yet I confess I often live for myself and follow my sinful desires. *Forgive me for rejecting who I am in Christ.*

You invite me into your peace, promising to lead me, protect me, and provide for me. Yet I confess I often plunge deeper into my anxious thoughts rather than draw near to your presence. *Forgive me for rejecting who I am in Christ.*

Silently reflect on the ways you have strayed from God's gracious authority. Confess aloud and receive God's free grace through Jesus.

surance

An invitation to receive the assurance of a new identity in the finished work of Christ.

Father, you promise, for the sake of your Son, to never leave me nor forsake me. I set my hope on your steadfast love. You have started a good work in me, and you are committed to finish it when Jesus returns. *Today, I receive your peace.*

Jesus, you are the Prince of Peace. You died in my place and made peace through the blood of your cross. You made me in your likeness and know me completely. You alone can tell me who I am. *Today, I receive your peace.*

Thanks be to God!

ipture Reading

The surrender to God's good and authoritative Word.

Paul, an apostle of Christ Jesus by the will of God, and Timothy our brother,

To the saints and faithful brothers in Christ at Colossae:

Grace to you and peace from God our Father.

We always thank God, the Father of our Lord Jesus Christ, when we pray for you, since we heard of your faith in Christ Jesus and of the love that you have for all the saints, because of the hope laid up for you in heaven. Of this you have heard before in the word of the truth, the gospel, which has come to you, as indeed in the whole world it is bearing fruit and increasing—as it also does among you, since the day you heard it and understood the grace of God in truth, just as you learned it from Epaphras our beloved fellow servant. He is a faithful minister of Christ on your behalf and has made known to us your love in the Spirit.

And so, from the day we heard, we have not ceased to pray for you, asking that you may be filled with the knowledge of his will in all spiritual wisdom and understanding, so as to walk in a manner worthy of the Lord, fully pleasing to him:

bearing fruit in every good work and increasing in the knowledge of God; being strengthened with all power, according to his glorious might, for all endurance and patience with joy; giving thanks to the Father, who has qualified you to shar in the inheritance of the saints in light. He has delivered us from the domain of darkness and transferred us to the kingdom of his beloved Son, in whom we ha redemption, the forgiveness of sins.

Colossians 1:1-14

Prayer

An invitation to bring the needs of our bodies, hearts, and minds to the care of God

Offer prayers for yourself and for others.

Benediction

A blessing from the authority of Scripture spoken over the people of God.
The following is based on Romans 8:38-39.

For I am sure that neither death nor life, nor angels nor rulers, nor things prese nor things to come, nor powers, nor height nor depth, nor anything else in all creation, will be able to separate me from the love of God in Christ Jesus my Lo
Send me now into the world as an image bearer of God.

Daily Liturgy: Week 7, Day 3

Identity and the Gospel

Call to Worship

An invitation from God to all humanity to behold and join the story, work, and eternal worship of Jesus. This prayer is based on Psalm 23.

The LORD is my shepherd; I shall not want. My very life is hidden in you. Because of your abundance, I lack nothing. My soul is restless until it finds rest in you. Beside your still waters, I find rest. You, Lord, are a fountain of living water. You overflow with life, and you pour your Spirit into me. Lead me in paths of righteousness for your name's sake. May your goodness and mercy go with me today. *Amen.*

Psalm

A SONG OF ASCENTS. OF DAVID.

If it had not been the LORD who was on our side—
let Israel now say—
if it had not been the LORD who was on our side
when people rose up against us,
then they would have swallowed us up alive,
when their anger was kindled against us;
then the flood would have swept us away,
the torrent would have gone over us;
then over us would have gone
the raging waters.

Blessed be the LORD,
who has not given us
as prey to their teeth!
We have escaped like a bird
from the snare of the fowlers;
the snare is broken,
and we have escaped!

Our help is in the name of the LORD,
who made heaven and earth.

Psalm 124

nfession

A call to acknowledge and forsake sin against God and one another.

Father, my one hope in life and in death is that I am not my own. My body and my soul belong to you. But I have listened to the voice of the world, and let it name me. *Father, forgive me and tune my ears to hear your voice.*

You have given me dignity and worth as your image bearer. But I have listened to the lie that my value comes from status and success. Remind me that the blood of your Son speaks a better word. *Father, forgive me and tune my ears to hear your voice.*

Silently reflect on the ways you have strayed from God's gracious authority. Confess aloud and receive God's free grace through Jesus.

;urance

An invitation to receive the assurance of a new identity in the finished work of Christ.

Jesus, you did not count equality with God a thing to be grasped, but you humbled yourself, taking the form of a servant. You lived a perfect life under the gaze of God, obeying him without wavering. You died my death, so I might live in your life. You rose again, and you are now seated at the right hand of the Father. You have surely borne my scars, and you will surely bring me home. This is my assurance and my hope. I am fully known by you alone, O Lord. *Thanks be to God!*

'ipture Reading

The surrender to God's good and authoritative Word.

He is the image of the invisible God, the firstborn of all creation. For by him all things were created, in heaven and on earth, visible and invisible, whether thrones or dominions or rulers or authorities—all things were created through him and for him. And he is before all things, and in him all things hold together. And he is the head of the body, the church. He is the beginning, the firstborn from the dead, that in everything he might be preeminent. For in him all the fullness of God was pleased to dwell, and through him to reconcile to himself all things, whether on earth or in heaven, making peace by the blood of his cross.

And you, who once were alienated and hostile in mind, doing evil deeds, he has now reconciled in his body of flesh by his death, in order to present you holy and blameless and above reproach before him, if indeed you continue in the faith, stable and steadfast, not shifting from the hope of the gospel that you heard, which has been proclaimed in all creation under heaven, and of which I, Paul, became a minister.

Colossians 1:15-23

Prayer

An invitation to bring the needs of our bodies, hearts, and minds to the care of God

Offer prayers for yourself and for others.

Benediction

A blessing from the authority of Scripture spoken over the people of God. The following is based on Philippians 4:7.

May the peace of God, which surpasses all understanding, guard my heart and mind in Christ Jesus. *Send me now into the world as an image bearer of God.*

Identity and the Gospel

Call to Worship

An invitation from God to all humanity to behold and join the story, work, and eternal worship of Jesus. This prayer is based on 1 Peter 2.

God, you have made us into a chosen race, a royal priesthood, a holy nation. We are a people of your possession, created to proclaim your excellencies. You hav called me out of darkness and into your marvelous light. Once, we were not a people, but now we are your people. Once, I had not received mercy, but now I overflow with your mercy. *Amen.*

Psalm

A SONG OF ASCENTS.

When the LORD restored the fortunes of Zion,
we were like those who dream.
Then our mouth was filled with laughter,
and our tongue with shouts of joy;
then they said among the nations,
"The LORD has done great things for them."
The LORD has done great things for us;
we are glad.

Restore our fortunes, O LORD,
like streams in the Negeb!
Those who sow in tears
shall reap with shouts of joy!
He who goes out weeping,
bearing the seed for sowing,
shall come home with shouts of joy,
bringing his sheaves with him.

Psalm 126

Daily Liturgy: Week 7, Day 4

fession

A call to acknowledge and forsake sin against God and one another.

Holy God, you made me out of the overflow of your love. I was made to reflect you in my relationship with others, but I have relied on my own strength and walked alone. *Forgive me, O God, for exalting myself above you.*

Holy God, you made me for your glory. I bear your image, and I only come to know myself as I find satisfaction in you. Yet I have looked to others to define me and fulfill me. *Forgive me, O God, for exalting others above you.*

Grant me the courage and humility to move toward others and make much of you.

Silently reflect on the ways you have strayed from God's gracious authority. Confess aloud and receive God's free grace through Jesus.

urance

An invitation to receive the assurance of a new identity in the finished work of Christ.

Father, I bring to mind your mercy, and I'm filled with hope. Through the cross and resurrection of Jesus, you brought me home from my wanderings. You've removed my mask, stripped my armor, and clothed me in the righteousness of Christ. You have called me your child, chosen and beloved. Because of you, I am made new and born again to a living hope. Jesus, you are my life, and I am most alive when I make my home in you. *Thanks be to God!*

pture Reading

The surrender to God's good and authoritative Word.

Now I rejoice in my sufferings for your sake, and in my flesh I am filling up what is lacking in Christ's afflictions for the sake of his body, that is, the church, of which I became a minister according to the stewardship from God that was given to me for you, to make the word of God fully known, the mystery hidden for ages and generations but now revealed to his saints. To them God chose to make known how great among the Gentiles are the riches of the glory of this mystery, which is Christ in you, the hope of glory. Him we proclaim, warning everyone and teaching everyone with all wisdom, that we may present everyone mature in Christ. For this I toil, struggling with all his energy that he powerfully works within me.

For I want you to know how great a struggle I have for you and for those at Laodicea and for all who have not seen me face to face, that their hearts may be encouraged, being knit together in love, to reach all the riches of full assurance of understanding and the knowledge of God's mystery, which is Christ, in whom are hidden all the treasures of wisdom and knowledge. I say this in order that no one may delude you with plausible arguments. For though I am absent in body, I am with you in spirit, rejoicing to see your good order and the firmness of you faith in Christ.

Colossians 1:24-2:5

Prayer

An invitation to bring the needs of our bodies, hearts, and minds to the care of God

Offer prayers for yourself and for others.

Benediction

A blessing from the authority of Scripture spoken over the people of God. The following is based on Revelation 1:5-6.

To him who loves me and has freed me from my sins by his blood and made us a kingdom, priests to his God and Father, to him be glory and dominion forever and ever. *Send me now into the world as an image bearer of God.*

Daily Liturgy: Week 7, Day 5

Identity and the Gospel

Call to Worship

An invitation from God to all humanity to behold and join the story, work, and etern worship of Jesus. This prayer is based on Colossians 1, Psalm 36, and Psalm 139.

Jesus, you are the image of the invisible God—to see you is to see the Father. All things were created by you, through you, and for you. You made me, knit me together, and called me wonderfully made. Your thoughts toward me are precio and vast. Your love toward me is rich and unending. I feast at your table and dri from the river of your delights. From you comes life and light. Jesus, you are my life, and I am most alive when I make my home in you. *Amen.*

Psalm

A SONG OF ASCENTS.

Remember, O LORD, in David's favor,
all the hardships he endured,
how he swore to the LORD
and vowed to the Mighty One of Jacob,
"I will not enter my house
or get into my bed,
I will not give sleep to my eyes
or slumber to my eyelids,
until I find a place for the LORD,
a dwelling place for the Mighty One of Jacob."

Behold, we heard of it in Ephrathah;
we found it in the fields of Jaar.
"Let us go to his dwelling place;
let us worship at his footstool!"

Arise, O LORD, and go to your resting place,
you and the ark of your might.
Let your priests be clothed with righteousness,
and let your saints shout for joy.
For the sake of your servant David,
do not turn away the face of your anointed one.

Psalm 132:1-10

Confession

You are the one who names me. But I confess I have fractured relationship with you by running from your will. Father, your presence is my home. I belong to you and with you. I confess I am often self-centered, self-protective, and self-reliant. *Forgive me and help me return to you.*

I wear my work and reputation as righteousness. I mask myself to fit in. I am a shapeshifter. But I was never meant to bear the weight of creating my own identity. Sin has left my heart fragmented and famished. *Forgive me and help me return to you.*

Silently reflect on the ways you have strayed from God's gracious authority. Confess aloud and receive God's free grace through Jesus.

Assurance

An invitation to receive the assurance of a new identity in the finished work of Christ.

In Christ, I am a new creation. The old has passed away; the new has come. In Jesus, I am no longer the person I was, or even the person I longed to become. As a beloved and adopted child of God, he invites me to take my place at his table. I am chosen and loved. I have been rescued from every enemy of my soul. Even now, my heart condemns me, but God is greater than my heart. Nothing can separate me from his love. *Thanks be to God!*

Scripture Reading

The surrender to God's good and authoritative Word.

Therefore, as you received Christ Jesus the Lord, so walk in him, rooted and built up in him and established in the faith, just as you were taught, abounding in thanksgiving.

See to it that no one takes you captive by philosophy and empty deceit, according to human tradition, according to the elemental spirits of the world, and not according to Christ. For in him the whole fullness of deity dwells bodily, and you have been filled in him, who is the head of all rule and authority. In him also you were circumcised with a circumcision made without hands, by putting off the body of the flesh, by the circumcision of Christ, having been buried with him in baptism, in which you were also raised with him through faith in the powerful working of God, who raised him from the dead. And you, who were dead in your trespasses and the uncircumcision of your flesh, God made alive together with him, having forgiven us all our trespasses, by canceling the record of debt that stood against us with its legal demands. This he set aside, nailing it to the cross. He disarmed the rulers and authorities and put them to open shame, by triumphing over them in him.

Colossians 2:6-15

Prayer

An invitation to bring the needs of our bodies, hearts, and minds to the care of God.

Offer prayers for yourself and for others.

Benediction

A blessing from the authority of Scripture spoken over the people of God. The following is based on Romans 11:33, 36.

Oh, the depth of the riches and wisdom and knowledge of God! How unsearchable are his judgments and how inscrutable his ways! For from him and through him and to him are all things. To him be glory forever. *Send me now into the world as an image bearer of God.*

Daily Liturgies: Week 8

Identity and the Gospel

Daily Liturgy: Week 8, Day 1

Identity and the Gospel

Call to Worship

An invitation from God to all humanity to behold and join the story, work, and eternal worship of Jesus. This prayer is based on Psalm 8, 16, and 139.

O LORD, my Lord. Your name is majestic, and your glory endures forever. Who am I that you are mindful of me? God, you are my maker. You have thoughtfully and wonderfully made me. You see me and know me. All your works are perfect. Those who seek you lack no good thing. Today, I seek you, Lord. You are my chosen portion and my cup. Because you have given me yourself, I have a beautiful inheritance. *Amen.*

Psalm

The LORD swore to David a sure oath
from which he will not turn back:
"One of the sons of your body
I will set on your throne.
If your sons keep my covenant
and my testimonies that I shall teach them,
their sons also forever
shall sit on your throne."

For the LORD has chosen Zion;
he has desired it for his dwelling place:
"This is my resting place forever;
here I will dwell, for I have desired it.
I will abundantly bless her provisions;
I will satisfy her poor with bread.
Her priests I will clothe with salvation,
and her saints will shout for joy.
There I will make a horn to sprout for David;
I have prepared a lamp for my anointed.
His enemies I will clothe with shame,
but on him his crown will shine."

Psalm 132:11-18

Daily Liturgy: Week 8, Day 1

nfession

A call to acknowledge and forsake sin against God and one another.

Father, you have made me in your image to reflect your glory. Yet I confess I regularly craft a false image and prefer to seek my own glory. *Forgive me for rejecting who I am in Christ.*

You have asked me to take up my cross, deny myself, and follow you. Yet I confess I often live for myself and follow my sinful desires. *Forgive me for rejecting who I am in Christ.*

You invite me into your peace, promising to lead me, protect me, and provide for me. Yet I confess I often plunge deeper into my anxious thoughts rather than draw near to your presence. *Forgive me for rejecting who I am in Christ.*

Silently reflect on the ways you have strayed from God's gracious authority. Confess aloud and receive God's free grace through Jesus.

surance

An invitation to receive the assurance of a new identity in the finished work of Christ.

Father, you promise, for the sake of your Son, to never leave me nor forsake me. I set my hope on your steadfast love. You have started a good work in me, and you are committed to finish it when Jesus returns. *Today, I receive your peace.*

Jesus, you are the Prince of Peace. You died in my place and made peace through the blood of your cross. You made me in your likeness and know me completely. You alone can tell me who I am. *Today, I receive your peace.*

Thanks be to God!

ripture Reading

The surrender to God's good and authoritative Word.

Therefore let no one pass judgment on you in questions of food and drink, or with regard to a festival or a new moon or a Sabbath. These are a shadow of the things to come, but the substance belongs to Christ. Let no one disqualify you, insisting on asceticism and worship of angels, going on in detail about visions, puffed up without reason by his sensuous mind, and not holding fast to the Head, from whom the whole body, nourished and knit together through its joints and ligaments, grows with a growth that is from God.

Daily Liturgy: Week 8, Day 1

If with Christ you died to the elemental spirits of the world, why, as if you were still alive in the world, do you submit to regulations— "Do not handle, Do not tas Do not touch" (referring to things that all perish as they are used)—according tc human precepts and teachings? These have indeed an appearance of wisdom i promoting self-made religion and asceticism and severity to the body, but they are of no value in stopping the indulgence of the flesh.

Colossians 2:16-23

Prayer

An invitation to bring the needs of our bodies, hearts, and minds to the care of God

Offer prayers for yourself and for others.

Benediction

A blessing from the authority of Scripture spoken over the people of God. The following is based on Romans 8:38-39.

For I am sure that neither death nor life, nor angels nor rulers, nor things preser nor things to come, nor powers, nor height nor depth, nor anything else in all creation, will be able to separate me from the love of God in Christ Jesus my Lor *Send me now into the world as an image bearer of God.*

Identity and the Gospel

Call to Worship

An invitation from God to all humanity to behold and join the story, work, and eternal worship of Jesus. This prayer is based on Psalm 23.

The LORD is my shepherd; I shall not want. My very life is hidden in you. Becaus of your abundance, I lack nothing. My soul is restless until it finds rest in you. Beside your still waters, I find rest. You, Lord, are a fountain of living water. You overflow with life, and you pour your Spirit into me. Lead me in paths of righteousness for your name's sake. May your goodness and mercy go with me today. *Amen.*

Psalm

Give thanks to the LORD, for he is good,
for his steadfast love endures forever.
Give thanks to the God of gods,
for his steadfast love endures forever.
Give thanks to the Lord of lords,
for his steadfast love endures forever;

to him who alone does great wonders,
for his steadfast love endures forever;
to him who by understanding made the heavens,
for his steadfast love endures forever;
to him who spread out the earth above the waters,
for his steadfast love endures forever;
to him who made the great lights,
for his steadfast love endures forever;
the sun to rule over the day,
for his steadfast love endures forever;
the moon and stars to rule over the night,
for his steadfast love endures forever;

to him who struck down the firstborn of Egypt,
for his steadfast love endures forever;
and brought Israel out from among them,
for his steadfast love endures forever;
with a strong hand and an outstretched arm,
for his steadfast love endures forever;
to him who divided the Red Sea in two,
for his steadfast love endures forever;
and made Israel pass through the midst of it,
for his steadfast love endures forever;

but overthrew Pharaoh and his host in the Red Sea,
for his steadfast love endures forever;
to him who led his people through the wilderness,
for his steadfast love endures forever;

Psalm 136:1-16

Confession

A call to acknowledge and forsake sin against God and one another.

Father, my one hope in life and in death is that I am not my own. My body and my soul belong to you. But I have listened to the voice of the world, and let it name me. *Father, forgive me and tune my ears to hear your voice.*

You have given me dignity and worth as your image bearer. But I have listened to the lie that my value comes from status and success. Remind me that the blood of your Son speaks a better word. *Father, forgive me and tune my ears to hear your voice.*

Silently reflect on the ways you have strayed from God's gracious authority. Confess aloud and receive God's free grace through Jesus.

ssurance

An invitation to receive the assurance of a new identity in the finished work of Christ.

Jesus, you did not count equality with God a thing to be grasped, but you humbled yourself, taking the form of a servant. You lived a perfect life under the gaze of God, obeying him without wavering. You died my death, so I might live in your life. You rose again, and you are now seated at the right hand of the Father. You have surely borne my scars, and you will surely bring me home. This is my assurance and my hope. I am fully known by you alone, O Lord. *Thanks be to God!*

cripture Reading

The surrender to God's good and authoritative Word.

If then you have been raised with Christ, seek the things that are above, where Christ is, seated at the right hand of God. Set your minds on things that are above, not on things that are on earth. For you have died, and your life is hidden with Christ in God. When Christ who is your life appears, then you also will appear with him in glory.

Colossians 3:1-4

Prayer

An invitation to bring the needs of our bodies, hearts, and minds to the care of God.

Offer prayers for yourself and for others.

Benediction

A blessing from the authority of Scripture spoken over the people of God.
The following is based on Philippians 4:7.

May the peace of God, which surpasses all understanding, guard my heart and my mind in Christ Jesus. *Send me now into the world as an image bearer of God.*

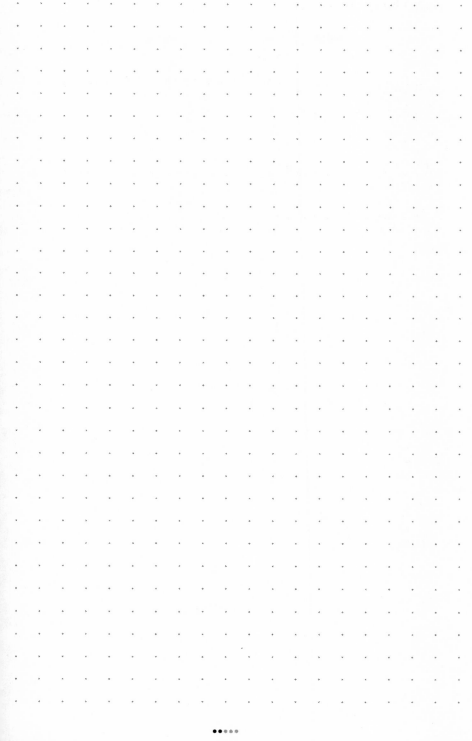

Identity and the Gospel

Call to Worship

An invitation from God to all humanity to behold and join the story, work, and eternal worship of Jesus. This prayer is based on 1 Peter 2.

God, you have made us into a chosen race, a royal priesthood, a holy nation. We are a people of your possession, created to proclaim your excellencies. You have called me out of darkness and into your marvelous light. Once, we were not a people, but now we are your people. Once, I had not received mercy, but now I overflow with your mercy. *Amen.*

Psalm

to him who struck down great kings,
for his steadfast love endures forever;
and killed mighty kings,
for his steadfast love endures forever;
Sihon, king of the Amorites,
for his steadfast love endures forever;
and Og, king of Bashan,
for his steadfast love endures forever;
and gave their land as a heritage,
for his steadfast love endures forever;
a heritage to Israel his servant,
for his steadfast love endures forever.

It is he who remembered us in our low estate,
for his steadfast love endures forever;
and rescued us from our foes,
for his steadfast love endures forever;
he who gives food to all flesh,
for his steadfast love endures forever.

Give thanks to the God of heaven,
for his steadfast love endures forever.

Psalm 136:17-26

nfession

A call to acknowledge and forsake sin against God and one another.

Holy God, you made me out of the overflow of your love. I was made to reflect you in my relationship with others, but I have relied on my own strength and walked alone. *Forgive me, O God, for exalting myself above you.*

Holy God, you made me for your glory. I bear your image, and I only come to know myself as I find satisfaction in you. Yet I have looked to others to define me and fulfill me. *Forgive me, O God, for exalting others above you.*

Grant me the courage and humility to move toward others and make much of you.

Silently reflect on the ways you have strayed from God's gracious authority. Confess aloud and receive God's free grace through Jesus.

surance

An invitation to receive the assurance of a new identity in the finished work of Christ.

Father, I bring to mind your mercy, and I'm filled with hope. Through the cross and resurrection of Jesus, you brought me home from my wanderings. You've removed my mask, stripped my armor, and clothed me in the righteousness of Christ. You have called me your child, chosen and beloved. Because of you, I am made new and born again to a living hope. Jesus, you are my life, and I am most alive when I make my home in you. *Thanks be to God!*

ripture Reading

The surrender to God's good and authoritative Word.

Put to death therefore what is earthly in you: sexual immorality, impurity, passion, evil desire, and covetousness, which is idolatry. On account of these the wrath of God is coming. In these you too once walked, when you were living in them. But now you must put them all away: anger, wrath, malice, slander, and obscene talk from your mouth. Do not lie to one another, seeing that you have put off the old self with its practices and have put on the new self, which is being renewed in knowledge after the image of its creator. Here there is not Greek and Jew, circumcised and uncircumcised, barbarian, Scythian, slave, free; but Christ is all, and in all.

Put on then, as God's chosen ones, holy and beloved, compassionate hearts, kindness, humility, meekness, and patience, bearing with one another and, if one has a complaint against another, forgiving each other; as the Lord has forgiven you, so you also must forgive. And above all these put on love, which binds everything together in perfect harmony. And let the peace of Christ rule in your hearts, to which indeed you were called in one body. And be thankful. Let the word of Christ dwell in you richly, teaching and admonishing one another in all wisdom, singing psalms and hymns and spiritual songs, with thankfulness in yo[ur] hearts to God. And whatever you do, in word or deed, do everything in the name of the Lord Jesus, giving thanks to God the Father through him.

Colossians 3:5-17

Prayer

An invitation to bring the needs of our bodies, hearts, and minds to the care of God.

Offer prayers for yourself and for others.

Benediction

A blessing from the authority of Scripture spoken over the people of God. The following is based on Revelation 1:5-6.

To him who loves me and has freed me from my sins by his blood and made us a kingdom, priests to his God and Father, to him be glory and dominion forever an[d] ever. *Send me now into the world as an image bearer of God.*

Daily Liturgy: Week 8, Day 4

Identity and the Gospel

Call to Worship

An invitation from God to all humanity to behold and join the story, work, and etern worship of Jesus. This prayer is based on Colossians 1, Psalm 36, and Psalm 139.

Jesus, you are the image of the invisible God—to see you is to see the Father. All things were created by you, through you, and for you. You made me, knit me together, and called me wonderfully made. Your thoughts toward me are precio and vast. Your love toward me is rich and unending. I feast at your table and dri from the river of your delights. From you comes life and light. Jesus, you are my life, and I am most alive when I make my home in you. *Amen.*

Psalm

A PSALM OF DAVID.

Hear my prayer, O LORD;
give ear to my pleas for mercy!
In your faithfulness answer me, in your righteousness!
Enter not into judgment with your servant,
for no one living is righteous before you.

For the enemy has pursued my soul;
he has crushed my life to the ground;
he has made me sit in darkness like those long dead.
Therefore my spirit faints within me;
my heart within me is appalled.

I remember the days of old;
I meditate on all that you have done;
I ponder the work of your hands.
I stretch out my hands to you;
my soul thirsts for you like a parched land. SELAH

Answer me quickly, O LORD!
My spirit fails!
Hide not your face from me,
lest I be like those who go down to the pit.
Let me hear in the morning of your steadfast love,
for in you I trust.
Make me know the way I should go,
for to you I lift up my soul.

Deliver me from my enemies, O LORD!

Daily Liturgy: Week 8, Day 4

I have fled to you for refuge.
Teach me to do your will,
for you are my God!
Let your good Spirit lead me
on level ground!

For your name's sake, O LORD, preserve my life!
In your righteousness bring my soul out of trouble!
And in your steadfast love you will cut off my enemies,
and you will destroy all the adversaries of my soul,
for I am your servant.

Psalm 143

nfession

A call to acknowledge and forsake sin against God and one another.

You are the one who names me. But I confess I have fractured relationship with you by running from your will. Father, your presence is my home. I belong to you and with you. I confess I am often self-centered, self-protective, and self-reliant. *Forgive me and help me return to you.*

I wear my work and reputation as righteousness. I mask myself to fit in. I am a shapeshifter. But I was never meant to bear the weight of creating my own identity. Sin has left my heart fragmented and famished. *Forgive me and help me return to you.*

Silently reflect on the ways you have strayed from God's gracious authority. Confess aloud and receive God's free grace through Jesus.

surance

An invitation to receive the assurance of a new identity in the finished work of Christ.

In Christ, I am a new creation. The old has passed away; the new has come. In Jesus, I am no longer the person I was, or even the person I longed to become. As a beloved and adopted child of God, he invites me to take my place at his table. I am chosen and loved. I have been rescued from every enemy of my soul. Even now, my heart condemns me, but God is greater than my heart. Nothing can separate me from his love. *Thanks be to God!*

Daily Liturgy: Week 8, Day 4

Scripture Reading

The surrender to God's good and authoritative Word.

Wives, submit to your husbands, as is fitting in the Lord. Husbands, love your wives, and do not be harsh with them. Children, obey your parents in everything for this pleases the Lord. Fathers, do not provoke your children, lest they becom discouraged. Bondservants, obey in everything those who are your earthly masters, not by way of eye-service, as people-pleasers, but with sincerity of hea fearing the Lord. Whatever you do, work heartily, as for the Lord and not for me knowing that from the Lord you will receive the inheritance as your reward. Yo are serving the Lord Christ. For the wrongdoer will be paid back for the wrong has done, and there is no partiality.

Masters, treat your bondservants justly and fairly, knowing that you also have a Master in heaven.

Colossians 3:18-4:1

Prayer

An invitation to bring the needs of our bodies, hearts, and minds to the care of God.

Offer prayers for yourself and for others.

Benediction

A blessing from the authority of Scripture spoken over the people of God.
The following is based on Romans 11:33, 36.

Oh, the depth of the riches and wisdom and knowledge of God! How unsearchab are his judgments and how inscrutable his ways! For from him and through him and to him are all things. To him be glory forever. *Send me now into the world as an image bearer of God.*

Daily Liturgy: Week 8, Day 5

Identity and the Gospel

Call to Worship

An invitation from God to all humanity to behold and join the story, work, and eternal worship of Jesus. This prayer is based on Psalms 8, 16, and 139.

O LORD, my Lord. Your name is majestic, and your glory endures forever. Who am I that you are mindful of me? God, you are my maker. You have thoughtfully and wonderfully made me. You see me and know me. All your works are perfect. Those who seek you lack no good thing. Today, I seek you, Lord. You are my chosen portion and my cup. Because you have given me yourself, I have a beautiful inheritance. *Amen.*

Psalm

Praise the LORD!
For it is good to sing praises to our God;
for it is pleasant, and a song of praise is fitting.
The LORD builds up Jerusalem;
he gathers the outcasts of Israel.
He heals the brokenhearted
and binds up their wounds.
He determines the number of the stars;
he gives to all of them their names.
Great is our Lord, and abundant in power;
his understanding is beyond measure.
The LORD lifts up the humble;
he casts the wicked to the ground.

Sing to the LORD with thanksgiving;
make melody to our God on the lyre!
He covers the heavens with clouds;
he prepares rain for the earth;
he makes grass grow on the hills.
He gives to the beasts their food,
and to the young ravens that cry.
His delight is not in the strength of the horse,
nor his pleasure in the legs of a man,
but the LORD takes pleasure in those who fear him,
in those who hope in his steadfast love.

Praise the LORD, O Jerusalem!
Praise your God, O Zion!
For he strengthens the bars of your gates;
he blesses your children within you.

Daily Liturgy: Week 8, Day 5

He makes peace in your borders;
he fills you with the finest of the wheat.
He sends out his command to the earth;
his word runs swiftly.
He gives snow like wool;
he scatters frost like ashes.
He hurls down his crystals of ice like crumbs;
who can stand before his cold?
He sends out his word, and melts them;
he makes his wind blow and the waters flow.
He declares his word to Jacob,
his statutes and rules to Israel.
He has not dealt thus with any other nation;
they do not know his rules.
Praise the LORD!

Psalm 147

nfession

A call to acknowledge and forsake sin against God and one another.

Father, you have made me in your image to reflect your glory. Yet I confess I regularly craft a false image and prefer to seek my own glory. *Forgive me for rejecting who I am in Christ.*

You have asked me to take up my cross, deny myself, and follow you. Yet I confess I often live for myself and follow my sinful desires. *Forgive me for rejecting who I am in Christ.*

You invite me into your peace, promising to lead me, protect me, and provide for me. Yet I confess I often plunge deeper into my anxious thoughts rather than draw near to your presence. *Forgive me for rejecting who I am in Christ.*

Silently reflect on the ways you have strayed from God's gracious authority. Confess aloud and receive God's free grace through Jesus.

Daily Liturgy: Week 8, Day 5

Assurance

An invitation to receive the assurance of a new identity in the finished work of Chr

Father, you promise, for the sake of your Son, to never leave me nor forsake me. set my hope on your steadfast love. You have started a good work in me, and yo are committed to finish it when Jesus returns. *Today, I receive your peace.*

Jesus, you are the Prince of Peace. You died in my place and made peace throug the blood of your cross. You made me in your likeness and know me completely. You alone can tell me who I am. *Today, I receive your peace.*

Thanks be to God!

Scripture Reading

The surrender to God's good and authoritative Word.

Continue steadfastly in prayer, being watchful in it with thanksgiving. At the sar time, pray also for us, that God may open to us a door for the word, to declare th mystery of Christ, on account of which I am in prison—that I may make it clear, which is how I ought to speak.

Walk in wisdom toward outsiders, making the best use of the time. Let your speech always be gracious, seasoned with salt, so that you may know how you ought to answer each person.

Tychicus will tell you all about my activities. He is a beloved brother and faithful minister and fellow servant in the Lord. I have sent him to you for this very purpose, that you may know how we are and that he may encourage your heart and with him Onesimus, our faithful and beloved brother, who is one of you. Th will tell you of everything that has taken place here.

Aristarchus my fellow prisoner greets you, and Mark the cousin of Barnabas (concerning whom you have received instructions—if he comes to you, welcom him), and Jesus who is called Justus. These are the only men of the circumcision among my fellow workers for the kingdom of God, and they have been a comfor to me. Epaphras, who is one of you, a servant of Christ Jesus, greets you, always struggling on your behalf in his prayers, that you may stand mature and fully assured in all the will of God. For I bear him witness that he has worked hard for you and for those in Laodicea and in Hierapolis. Luke the beloved physician greets you, as does Demas. Give my greetings to the brothers at Laodicea, and t Nympha and the church in her house. And when this letter has been read amon you, have it also read in the church of the Laodiceans; and see that you also reac the letter from Laodicea. And say to Archippus, "See that you fulfill the ministry that you have received in the Lord."

Daily Liturgy: Week 8, Day 5

I, Paul, write this greeting with my own hand. Remember my chains. Grace be with you.

Colossians 4:2-18

Prayer

An invitation to bring the needs of our bodies, hearts, and minds to the care of God.

Offer prayers for yourself and for others.

Benediction

A blessing from the authority of Scripture spoken over the people of God. The following is based on Romans 8:38-39.

For I am sure that neither death nor life, nor angels nor rulers, nor things present nor things to come, nor powers, nor height nor depth, nor anything else in all creation, will be able to separate me from the love of God in Christ Jesus my Lord. *Send me now into the world as an image bearer of God.*

Made in the USA
Coppell, TX
10 September 2023

21433196R00127